Caroline de Margerie has worked as a diplomat and is now a member of the Conseil d'Etat, the supreme administrative court in France. Her first book was a biography of Edmond Rostand, the author of *Cyrano de Bergerac*. She lives in Paris.

Frances FitzGerald is a journalist and the author of several works of nonfiction, including the Pulitzer Prize– and National Book Award–winning *Fire in the Lake*. She has also received the Bancroft Prize for history, the National Academy of Arts and Sciences Award, and the *Los Angeles Times* Award for nonfiction, among others. She is Susan Mary Alsop's goddaughter.

Christopher Murray is an American musicologist and translator based in Paris.

Praise for *American Lady*

"This is not just an exquisitely perceptive portrait of a remarkable woman, it is a beautifully painted conversation piece including many of the great figures from a privileged age of elegance and intelligence."
—Antony Beevor, bestselling author of *The Second World War*

"Written with a verve and clarity that her subject would both admire and regret, *American Lady* captures the charms, contradictions, and convictions that put Susan Mary Alsop at the crossroads of society, politics, and glamorous love affairs in Paris, Washington, and her other ports of call. Many of the great men—and women—of her time gravitated to Susan Mary's movable salon to take in each other, and their ever resourceful hostess. It's all here."
—Jim Hoagland, contributing editor, *The Washington Post*

"Susan Mary Alsop was a cool, beautiful mixture of public discretion and private daring. On two continents and over four decades she invited the world's most powerful people to her homes, facilitating, networking, connecting. Caroline de Margerie's *American Lady* is as sharp and stylish as its fascinating subject."   —Stacy A. Cordery, author of *Alice: Alice Roosevelt Longworth, from White House Princess to Washington Power Broker*

"The history of postwar Europe and America told through the prism of power and privilege. A most enjoyable book about a most elegant lady."
—Jane Stanton Hitchcock, author of *Mortal Friends*

"Once upon a time the coolest people in the world were Americans. From the era of F. Scott Fitzgerald through that of *Mad Men*, they set the scene for the age of Camelot and not a few of its most consequential confrontations. No one better exemplified this rarefied and influential species than Susan Mary Alsop, whose eventful, thoughtful, complex, and passionate life Caroline de Margerie brilliantly chronicles in this exquisitely researched, impossible to put down biography." —Thomas Caplan, author of *The Spy Who Jumped Off the Screen*

"Like Jackie Kennedy, Susan Mary Alsop was the kind of American aristocrat who survived with her wits and good manners. . . . Author Caroline de Margerie deftly chronicles the life of a woman who gave little away emotionally but whose range of experience—including discreet romantic dramas with consecutive British ambassadors—speaks for itself."
    —Cherie Burns, author of *Searching for Beauty: The Life of Millicent Rogers*

"Feminine insights into the life of this fascinating woman." —*Chicago Tribune*

"At its heart, this engaging, gentle biography is a tale of how a particular slice of the other half lived. . . . A one-woman *Downton Abbey*."
    —Associated Press

"Caroline de Margerie avoids hagiography, instead depicting a fabulously interesting, complicated and influential woman."   —*Chicago Tribune*

"The first-ever biography of the Georgetown doyenne charts her life from Paris—where she charmed Winston Churchill and was a favorite of Christian Dior—to Washington D.C., where she threw some of the best parties of the Camelot era."   —*The Wall Street Journal*

"[De Margerie] goes behind the facade to reveal a passionate personality torn between her sense of duty and her personal desires. . . . De Margerie had access to some five hundred previously unseen letters."   —*Women's Wear Daily*

"An engrossing, perceptive, and nuanced portrait of a celebrated socialist who once knew everyone worth knowing."   —*Publishers Weekly*

"Thin, fashionable, well informed, yet a little wicked, Susan Mary had what it took to be talked about, and the Alsops' gatherings were the talk of Georgetown's 'glory years.' Paris-based author de Margerie paints in bold, bright outlines the compelling story of this Jamesian heroine. Entertaining story of a dynamic literary woman who sparked a fascinating life from the changing currents of the age."   —*Kirkus Reviews*

"Compact, entertaining . . . De Margerie colorfully unpacks the details of Alsop's life."   —*The Washingtonian*

"The story of a determined, pedigreed woman. . . . A saloniste extraordinaire."
    —*The Washington Times*

American Lady

THE LIFE OF
SUSAN MARY ALSOP

CAROLINE DE MARGERIE

INTRODUCTION BY FRANCES FITZGERALD

TRANSLATED BY CHRISTOPHER MURRAY

PENGUIN BOOKS

PENGUIN BOOKS

Published by the Penguin Group
Penguin Group (USA) LLC
375 Hudson Street
New York, New York 10014

USA | Canada | UK | Ireland | Australia | New Zealand | India | South Africa | China
penguin.com
A Penguin Random House Company

First published in the United States of America by Viking Penguin,
a member of Penguin Group (USA) Inc., 2012
Published in Penguin Books 2013

Originally published in French as *American Lady: Une reporter en gants blancs*
by Editions Robert Laffont, Paris.

Acknowledgment is made to Bill Patten for permission to use
photographs on insert page 5, top, left and right.

THE LIBRARY OF CONGRESS HAS CATALOGED THE HARDCOVER EDITION AS FOLLOWS:
Margerie, Caroline de.
[American lady. English]
American lady : the life of Susan Mary Alsop / Caroline de Margerie ; translated by
Christopher Murray.
p. cm.
Includes bibliographical references and index.
ISBN 978-0-670-02574-9 (hc.)
ISBN 978-0-14-312413-9 (pbk.)
1. Alsop, Susan Mary. 2. Upper-class women—United States—Biography. 3. Upper class—United
States—Biography. 4. Socialites—United States—Biography. 5. Alsop, Susan Mary—Friends and
associates. 6. Americans—France—Paris—Biography. 7. United States—Biography. 8. Paris
(France)—Biography. 9. Political culture—Washington (D.C.)—History—20th century.
10. Washington (D.C.)—Social life and customs—20th century. I. Title.
CT275.A6228M3713 2012
975.3'04092—dc23
[B]   2012003424

Printed in the United States of America
3 5 7 9 10 8 6 4 2

To our beloved children, Stanislas, Pierre, and Éléonore,

Jean-Rodolphe, Donatella, and Alexandra

This book was completed with the help of Aniela Vilgrain.

Contents

Introduction

One evening in October 1962 Susan Mary and Joe Alsop gave a
small dinner for Chip Bohlen, the State Department's leading
authority on the Soviet Union, who was leaving Washington to
become ambassador in Paris. The President and Mrs. Kennedy
came, and dinner was badly delayed because the president took
Bohlen into the garden and walked up and down with him for a
long time. Susan Mary worried. Chip's wife Avis had a bad back,
the leg of lamb was drying up in the oven, and it wasn't like the
president to conduct business before dinner. They finally came in,
and dinner was served, but then Susan Mary noticed two other
unusual things. Twice that evening the president asked Bohlen
and the other Russian expert there, Isaiah Berlin, what happened
in history when the Russians found themselves in awkward situ-
ations from which it would be difficult to extricate themselves.
"This startled me," Susan Mary later wrote, "for Kennedy was the
best extractor of information I ever met, and I was most surprised
that he wanted to go back for more on a subject that didn't even
seem interesting." Her other impression of him, she wrote, was

physical. "That night he was revved up—I wish I could think of a better simile. It seemed to me that a very powerful engine, say Bentley or Ferrari, beside which I had the honor of sitting many times, running at fifty miles an hour, had been thrown into the intensity of full power, controlled, the throttle was out and, what was more, he was enjoying it. It was thrilling, like sitting by lightning, but it made no sense. My mind struggled to comprehend, but the news had been very commonplace that week and I couldn't imagine what made me say to Joe as we went to bed that something was up, for sure."

It was. That morning President Kennedy had been shown the first CIA reconnaissance photographs of the Russian missiles sites in Cuba.*

Susan Mary became a historian in her sixties. Before that she would have described herself as a housewife, but she was always a writer, and she often had a front seat to the making of history of her own time. With her first husband, Bill Patten, an attaché to the U.S. embassy in Paris, she lived through the dramas of France from the end of World War II to the crisis in Algeria that ushered in the Fifth Republic and the presidency of Charles de Gaulle. Her marriage to the columnist Joseph Alsop in 1961 brought her back to Washington and into the inner circles of the Kennedy administration. Like the heroine of Henry Adams's *Democracy*, she then made her own place in Georgetown society. Invitations to her parties were sought after by the foreign policy makers of subsequent administrations—as well as by European statesmen and intellectuals. She found this all perfectly normal. She was,

---

* *To Marietta from Paris 1945–1960*, pp. 42–43.

after all, a Jay, the daughter of a veteran diplomat and a descendant of John Jay, one of the founding fathers of the United States.

In the cosmopolitan life she led, Susan Mary came to know an astonishing array of people, ranging from Winston Churchill to Evelyn Waugh, and from Isaiah Berlin to Christian Dior. Her friends included Walter Lippmann, Paul Reynaud, Jean Cocteau, Henry Kissinger and the Duke and Duchess of Windsor. She met Ho Chi Minh and General de Gaulle. And she wrote about all of them brilliantly in her letters. David Bruce, the distinguished American diplomat, wrote of her collected letters that they reminded him irresistibly of the letters of Madame de Sévigné. Susan Mary thought of herself as an observer but she herself was as remarkable a character as any she observed. Her life was never an easy one—not as a child and not in her two marriages—but, relentlessly energetic, highly intelligent, and charismatic, she overcame most of the troubles it sent her—and rarely spoke of them. Frail looking but physically strong, I think of her as one of those small focused birds that (unbeknownst to most of us) fly thousands of miles every year from their winter to their summer habitat and back.

My acquaintance with Susan Mary began early. She and my mother, Marietta, became friends—friends for life—in the late 1930s when as teenagers they spent summers together on Mount Desert Island, Maine. Susan Mary's family had a house in Bar Harbor, then a fashionable resort for grand families from the Pulitzers to the Potter Palmers. Franklin D. Roosevelt visited, as did Jane Addams, the Chicago reformer. Marietta, the daughter and granddaughter of New England clergymen, far preferred Bar Harbor to the small summer community across the island where her Peabody family had a house. She wanted to live in the big world, and Susan Mary Jay, though painfully shy, was a part of it. In summers, freed from their boarding schools, the two went through the trials of the debutante parties together. Marietta met my father, Desmond FitzGerald, in Bar Harbor, and while they were engaged, my father introduced Susan Mary to his friend from Harvard Bill Patten. Bill and Susan Mary were married in 1939 within months of my parents—the two women just twenty-two and their husbands "older men" in their early thirities. Susan Mary became my godmother when I was born a year later, and to my eternal gratitude she took the job seriously all of her life. She sent Christmas presents every year—often a book she liked —and always kept up with me, if not in person, then through Marietta or in letters.

When the United States entered the war in 1941, most of the men Susan Mary knew went off to war and scattered around the world. Bill had serious asthma and to his great chagrin had to take a desk job in Washington. Desie, as my father was called, joined the army as a private, but went through officer training and in early 1944 found himself in Burma as the adviser to a Chinese battalion trained in India. Knowing how important letters were to soldiers far from home, Susan Mary wrote to him—as doubtless to others—every few months. Her letters did not survive the monsoon rains and the constant marching, but she kept some of his return letters, and from them one can see what a wonderful correspondent she was even then. Excerpts from one of Desie's letters show her range of interests.

"Somewhere in Burma" 20 April 1944

Dear Soozle [a pet name she later abandoned]
    Your delightful letter of March 25 arrived today . . .
My promptness in replying isn't in the least typical of
me, but your letters give me such pleasure that I am
inspired to seize the nearest chunk of papyrus . . .
    What you say about the newspapers' idea of the
geography of Burma is vividly truthful . . . Frequently
between the Sunday Times and Monday Herald [Tri-
bune] I find I have migrated a couple of hundred miles
and crossed a range of mountains . . . all of this quite
painlessly.
    Your life in Washington with New York interludes
sounds very gay and crowded with cosmic characters.
I think your attitude about the Balkans is quite reasonable. I would suggest that a section of Libya be
roped off for their future quarrels . . .

In another letter dated December 19, 1944 Desie wrote:

    Your letters are a joy and your sketches of our
friends very deft and amusing. What is more, they
leave me feeling as if I had seen them again myself . . .
    M. [Marietta] tells me that Bill is off to Paris and
that you will follow in a few months. That sounds perfect for the combined Patten talents. We count on Bill
[to return the franc to its former condition] and you to
make the French a nation of USophiles."

Bill and Susan Mary went to Paris—he as the economic attaché
to the American embassy and she determined to help his career
and to get to know France. Two years later my parents divorced—
their marriage one of the many casualties of long separation during the war—and both remarried afterwards. Happily Susan
Mary got along famously with my English stepfather, Ronald
Tree, whom she had met before he married Marietta. The two
shared passionate interests in art, architecture, and British politics. In the immediate postwar years she and Bill spent weekends
at Ditchley, the Georgian house he had in Oxfordshire. Later she
often came to stay with us in New York or in the house Ronnie
had built in Barbados. She also remained friends with Desie, who
had joined the CIA and settled in Washington. So our lives remained entwined.

In Paris, away from her domineering mother, Susan Mary
flourished. Bill's asthma often debilitated him and prevented him
from advancing in the foreign service, but Susan Mary had
enough energy and ambition for two. Like many women of her
time, she never went to college, but she educated herself in French
literature and politics, art, architecture, and foreign affairs. She
made friends in what most other Americans considered the impenetrable society of French aristocrats and intellectuals. She also
made important English friends, among them Duff Cooper, then
the ambassador to Paris, and the love of her life. In her frequent
letters to Marietta she described the privations of France after the
war and the events she witnessed from the trial of Marshal Pétain
to the opening of Dior's first collection. ("Going into the fitting
rooms," she wrote, "was more dangerous than entering a den of

female lions before feeding time . . ."*) Later she described meeting Raymond Aron, the renowned political scientist: "He is tiny, birdlike, electric, with a thin big nose and long fingers, which he curls and uncurls when someone else is talking, not because he doesn't want to hear what they have to say but because his quick mind has caught the other's thought from the first words and he wants him to get on with it."† She also relayed the account of a meeting at Matignon between the prime ministers of Britain and France at a tense moment in Anglo-French relations. The British prime minister, Harold Macmillan, arriving hours late, made a speech about the failure of the Greek city-states to band together against Philip of Macedon. The moral, she wrote, was obvious, but Macmillan, carried away by his subject, began to speak in ancient Greek, and other members of the delegation outdid each other in quotations from Demosthenes about the disastrous disaccords of the Achaean and Delian leagues. At last, Gladwyn Jebb, the ambassador to France, and one of the best performers, noticed the growing indignation of the French.‡

Susan Mary also described what now seems an antique civilization in which Europeans of the *grand monde* gave elaborate picnics in the countryside and costume balls, where everyone danced until five in the morning. (Today the rich build houses half as big as Versailles with Jacuzzis in every bathroom, but they never seem to entertain, much less give balls.) The most extravagant of these

---

* *To Marietta from Paris, 1945–1960*, p. 93.
† Ibid., p. 307.
‡ Ibid., p. 310.

parties was Charles de Bestegui's 1951 masked ball in Venice, where the guests came in eighteenth-century costumes to match his eighteenth-century palazzo and its Tiepolo frescoes. Susan Mary, who drove down from Paris with Bill, wrote Marietta: "We first encountered the party in the courtyard of the Beau-Rivage hotel in Lausanne, where we spent the night. At 9 a.m. it was full of chauffeurs strapping and re-strapping Dior boxes to the tops of basketwork Rolls-Royces in preparation for the Simplon Pass, which we crossed in what I can only describe as a human chain of Reboux hatboxes."*

Summers, Susan Mary would sometimes go to Mount Desert to visit her mother, and if Desie was there on one of his short vacations from what we called "the pickle factory" (aka the CIA) the two would hike together. Desie, who had marched across Burma and up through China, had a long stride, and only Susan Mary could keep up with him. They would pack sandwiches and walk across the mountains from one side of the island to the other talking nonstop.

Susan Mary had a talent for friendship. She didn't suffer "tedious" people who went on about their illnesses or their domestics, and she preferred those who led more worldly lives. But the attachments she made were strong. Her several close women friends—Marietta, Marina Sulzberger, Dottie Kidder, Elise Bordeaux-Groult, and others—claimed her attention no matter what else she was doing. She looked after them in sickness or in sorrow, and they in turn took care of her. She once said that she made a better friend than a wife or a mother, and possibly that was

---

* *To Marietta from Paris, 1945–1960*, p. 183.

true. All the same, I remember her and Bill as more child friendly than many couples my mother knew. In those days Americans in Europe used to send their young children off with the nanny to beach resorts on the English Channel for a couple of weeks every summer. It was thought to be good for them. Susan Mary did that when her two children, Billy and Anne, were small, but to her credit she sometimes endured the fog and freezing water with them. Bill, whom I remember as a handsome man with a sweet smile, adored children, even when they weren't behaving well. Susan Mary had less talent than Bill for engaging the very young, but she had the generous, if disconcerting, habit of treating children over eight as if they had something interesting to say.

After Bill died in early 1960, Joe Alsop, an old friend of hers and Bill's, proposed to her. According to de Margerie, he not only offered her a marvelous life in Washington but admitted that he was a homosexual and seemed to reveal a lonely, vulnerable person beneath his tough exterior. The message—or the message she read—was that he needed her, and that with her he might change. Marietta later told me that she had implored her friend not to marry Joe. Yes, he was a brilliant journalist and cultivated man, but in addition to being a closeted homosexual, he was a confirmed bachelor and something of a tyrant. "Marry the man today and change his ways tomorrow"—Adelaide's line in *Guys and Dolls*—was, Marietta said, one of the worst pieces of advice ever given. Susan Mary, however, married Joe, and for some years it seemed that Marietta had been wrong.

I was abroad during the Kennedy years, but the novelist Ward Just, then working for *Newsweek*, dined with the Alsops several times in that period and remembers the dinners as marvelous.

There would always be men like Chip Bohlen, Robert McNamara or McGeorge Bundy and their wives plus a couple of young reporters or foreign service officers. Joe, benign, at one end of the dinner table, would draw out his important guests, often seeming to be conducting a tutorial for the younger men with the flattering implication that they would one day become a part of the august establishment that ran American foreign policy. Susan Mary at the other end of the table would always see to it that everyone was included in the conversation. She was, Ward thought, the best of hostesses, attractive and sexy, with a twinkle in her eye.

In those days Joe was in top form. He was pleased with the progressive shift in Washington on domestic issues, particularly civil rights, and he was uncharacteristically optimistic about U.S. prospects in the Cold War. Even while writing his weekly columns he managed to finish a book on one of his other great interests, the archaeology of the Greek Bronze Age. His mood, however, changed with the growing disaster in Vietnam. He had always been a hawk on Vietnam—once taking credit for having invented the "domino theory" and always pounding on in his column about the need for an expansion of the war. Some, only partly in jest, said that Lyndon Johnson had committed regular troops to the war because he was afraid of Alsop. Having served with General Claire Chenault in the China-Burma theater during World War II, Joe saw Vietnam through the lenses of the war with Japan. Throughout the sixties he made one or two trips to Vietnam every year, meeting only with the ranking generals, flying in their aircraft and reporting that the United States was winning the war. He refused to hear any evidence to the contrary, even when it came from well-informed old friends. As time went on, he grew more and more adamant. At dinner at the Alsop house in the mid-sixties, I and a friend of mine had the temerity (and the stupidity) of youth to challenge one of his sweeping pronouncements. He roared so that his ancestral portraits shook on the walls. It got worse. As American casualties mounted and there was still no light at the end of the tunnel, he accused fellow journalists and antiwar congressmen of seeking an American defeat. (Privately he even accused one of them of working for the KGB.) His years of reporting on Vietnam were nothing but ashes, and somewhere he knew it. The Alsop dinner parties became nightmares, with Joe drinking too much and Susan Mary sitting in anguished silence at her end of the table.

Susan Mary bore the brunt of Joe's anger and frustration. She never said a word about it except to Marietta and perhaps to one or two other intimate friends. In company she defended Joe and even seemed to endorse his untenable positions about the war. I thought of her as a victim of the Stockholm syndrome. How cruel he was to her I find out only now, but I saw the consequences. Her hard-won self-confidence disappeared, and she put up a brittle front where it used to be: anything but appear pathetic or less than a great conversationalist. She tried so hard that even her voice sounded unnatural. The marriage lasted until 1973—far too long—but clearly she loved Joe, for she continued to see him frequently afterwards. Both of them were much better off as friends.

Susan Mary moved into a Watergate apartment and in its anonymous surroundings began to make a new life for herself. In 1975 she published an edited version of her letters to Marietta from Paris 1945–1960. The book showed off her wit and style, and now that the world she wrote about has disappeared, Atlantis-like, into the distant past, it reads even better than it did at the time. There's a nugget for historians on almost every page. The book was well received, and encouraged, Susan Mary took up writing in earnest and published three books of history within a decade. When her sight failed to the point where she could no longer do extensive research, she became a contributing editor of *Architectural Digest* and wrote about architecture, gardens and interior design. She worked hard and loved it.

Susan Mary's mother died in 1977 at the age of ninety-eight and, as de Margerie writes, unlamented. Even in her last years as an invalid the old lady never stopped talking—or making it clear to everyone that she was the center of the universe and that only her wishes counted. By then Susan Mary was actually able to say that she found her mother "tiresome." (She told me her mother was 103, and I believed her, not realizing the number was a metaphor.) In any case, Susan Mary finally inherited the house she loved in Northeast Harbor, Maine. Bought by her mother sometime after the 1947 fire devastated Bar Harbor, the house had been built by Charles William Eliot, the famous late-nineteenth-century president of Harvard. A white shingled house on the top of a bluff overlooking the sea, it had well-proportioned rooms full of light and air. Susan Mary painted it in pale colors and furnished the living room with comfortable chintz-covered sofas and reading chairs. A wide window opened onto a view of islands and sailboats tacking across the Western Way. She also inherited a house in Georgetown—well described by de Margerie—and resumed a hectic social life. In the early 1990s I stayed with her often there on reporting trips. She'd grill me about the person I'd just interviewed or tell me what she'd learned about a famous house before rushing off to a dinner party on Embassy Row. She had more time in Maine, where life was relatively simple. My husband, a newspaper man, amused her, and when we went for a walk or dined with her, she would tell us wonderful stories about figures like Sumner Welles or about Bar Harbor when she and Marietta were young. (If only I had written them down!)

In her last summer in Maine I read to her. As the summer drew to a close, we were finishing Walter Isaacson's biography of Benjamin Franklin when I came across a paragraph quoting her description of the French foreign minister, the Comte de Vergennes, in what Isaacson said was her "delightful portrayal of the period" in *Yankees at the Court*.* I know she was thrilled, but she wouldn't say so. Similarly, were she alive today, I think she would be thrilled by *An American Lady*. She would have to admire the depth of de Margerie's research and the clarity of her style—and perhaps she would even have to admit to the acuity of de Margerie's insights into the main character. Still, because she was trained not to take center stage, she would never say so.

---

* As quoted in Walter Isaacson, *Benjamin Franklin: An American Life* (New York: Simon & Schuster, 2004), p. 337.

The Jays

John Jay

Benjamin Franklin and John Jay made a good team. Wearing fur hats and cotton hose, Franklin wooed Parisian salons that delighted in his rustic appearance and the tremendous eloquence he displayed in the cause of the American colonies' independence. John Jay was less of a charmer and did not much like the French despite his French ancestry (his grandfather Pierre-Auguste Jay, a Huguenot, had fled religious persecution and settled in America around the end of the seventeenth century). But he was an experienced diplomat who sheltered behind his government's instructions when he needed to and calmly disregarded them when he felt he knew best. He successfully negotiated the Treaty of Independence, which was signed by him, Franklin, and John Adams in Paris on September 3, 1783. This diplomatic feat won him the distinction of being one of the Founding Fathers of the young American Republic, and made him the first chief justice of the United States.

No other member of the Jay family would match John Jay's prestige and national importance; nevertheless, thanks to him, the Jays found themselves at the summit of America's aristocracy of merit, a position they would maintain throughout the nineteenth century and that their twentieth-century descendant Susan Mary would view with pride and a sense of obligation. The men of the family studied law at Columbia, Yale, or Harvard before becoming bankers or lawyers distinguished by restraint and lack of greed. They were occasionally sent on diplomatic missions and they all had a sense of civic responsibility, often serving on hospital or university boards or taking part in local assemblies. Several of these quiet, law-abiding citizens became known as outspoken abolitionists. A number of them chose to live in New York City or in the Hudson River Valley, where the most respectable and affluent families owned estates as vast as those of Virginia planters.

Wealth, necessary for leading a comfortable life in public service, came through marriage to powerful clans such as the Bayards, the Van Cortlandts, the Livingstons, and the Astors. In 1876, Augustus Jay, John Jay's great-grandson, married Emily Kane, the great-granddaughter of John Jacob Astor, who had once owned entire swaths of the island of Manhattan. Attractive Emily, rumored to put rouge on her nipples like a saloon girl, made a hit in Paris, where her husband took a position as a diplomat soon after their marriage. Two sons were born: Peter Augustus in 1877 and Delancey in 1881.

Diplomatic Wanderings

Peter followed in his father's footsteps, attending Harvard and choosing to become a diplomat. President Theodore Roosevelt, a friend of his parents, appointed him to his first post in October 1902, recommending that the young man take his job seriously.

The young man obeyed, although he never forgot to have a pleasant time. He served in Paris, Constantinople—where he played polo on the shores of the Bosporus—Tokyo, and Cairo. A few months before war broke out in Europe, he was sent to Rome with his wife and daughter.

It would be unseemly to speculate whether Peter's marriage to Susan Alexander McCook, which took place in 1909 in New York, had been a love match. Susan came from a family famous for having sent seventeen men to fight on the Union side in the Civil War. Unlike her forebears, she had little taste for adventure or affection for daredevils and hotheads. She was a sensible and composed woman who soon became her husband's best adviser. Two years after the wedding, their first daughter, Emily, was born. Seven years later, on June 19, 1918, in Rome, they had their second daughter, Susan Mary.

After six years in Rome, the world tour picked up again: El Salvador for a couple of insipid months, then Bucharest. Peter's job was to defend the interests of American companies exploiting Romanian petroleum, a resource whose production had taken off after a difficult period during the war. In his free time, he escorted the Romanian queen, Marie, a granddaughter of both Czar Alexander II and Queen Victoria, who was often photographed as a Byzantine icon dripping with jewels or as an operetta peasant girl in an embroidered blouse and head scarf. They spoke French together and rode at dawn in the woods of the queen's country estate at Sinaia or along the tree-lined paths of Cismigiu Gardens in Bucharest.

Meanwhile, Peter Jay's family kept to their residence, a massive and graceless house saved only by a fountain-ornamented garden in which Susan Mary toddled about, a sturdy little girl dressed in white cambric, holding on tightly to the hand of her older sister. Emily looked every inch the perfect child with her blue tunic and ringlets.

In 1926, Peter Jay was sent to Argentina as ambassador. The entire family liked Buenos Aires. At fifteen, Emily was finally free of her governess and not yet of marriageable age. She took guitar lessons and invited her friends to parties at the embassy. Susan Mary was still too little to join in, and had to be satisfied by stolen glimpses of the pink and gold fetes where young girls, voluptuous and innocent, danced with one another.

One evening in December, not long before Christmas, Emily complained of a stomachache. She was taken to the hospital, where she underwent an appendectomy. When Emily returned home, the two sisters were kept apart. Susan Mary was shut up in her bedroom as if she had been naughty. Unhappy and bored, she could hear sounds, doors opening and closing, whispering in the corridors. Her nanny stopped scolding her. Her mother did not come to supervise her evening prayers. On December 20, silence gripped the house as night fell. The following day, the noises began again. It seemed as though the house were full of people moving the furniture around. Were they getting the place ready for a ball, Susan Mary wondered, or perhaps packing up? Only Emily could tell and Emily could not be asked.

Shortly thereafter, on December 30, the *Pan America* set sail for New York. On board were a coffin, two devastated parents, and a miserable little girl.

Alone

Immediately after Emily's death, Peter retired from diplomatic service and did not seek another occupation. He and his wife concentrated on their loss rather than on their remaining daughter. They lived in Washington and often spent time in Maine, where they had a house in Bar Harbor on Mount Desert Island. They rarely went out. Peter had his books and a worsening cough; Susan had a household to run and orders to give. They pretended to be busy, hiding their unutterable grief from each other.

Susan Mary knew that her parents, her father especially, made a sincere effort to take an interest in her work and play. But they always seemed distracted, and their gaze would drift away. She tried not to dwell on this, and did her best to fill up the space left vacant by Emily's absence. Because docility seemed to be the key to the adult universe, she gave up whims and tantrums as though they were toys she had outgrown. Formerly a headstrong child, she became yielding and considerate. The love of the young and humble can assume heroic proportions. In dedicating herself to her parents' consolation, Susan Mary was proffering tenderness that she knew would have no effect. Emily's name was never spoken, and Susan Mary learned to keep silent.

The lonely little girl took solace in books. She also liked playing on the shores of the icy-cold ocean, which she could see from her bedroom window in Maine. In 1932, at age fourteen, she was sent to Foxcroft, a girls' boarding school in Virginia with a vague but admirable program of sport (riding especially), etiquette, and academic studies. She applied herself as she always had, and graduated with honors in June 1935. She had made a few friends, acquired a measure of confidence, and perfected her sense of discipline. She was ready to make her entrance into the world and do what was expected of her. Almost.

On the Edge of Life

Night and Day

So the season started. A seemingly innocent notion, the season concealed a strictly regulated machine that dictated social interaction among upper-class children, ensuring that when the time came, they would be paired off according to the combined laws of attraction and the maintenance of wealth and tradition. The Great Depression had done little to reduce the expense or simplify the complexity of the rites, which remained nearly identical to those practiced in England, apart from the presentation at court.

Still, it was not an entirely disagreeable system. The mothers kept a watchful eye, the fathers paid the bills, and the children danced the night away. It was a charmed moment in life: pleasure was the only duty, and choosing among dozens of engraved invitations the only task. There were parties in blue and white tents on the sweeping lawns of Long Island, teas in Boston, dinner dances in Philadelphia, and long evenings in New York that lasted until the pale light of dawn beckoned to bed. Night was no longer the opposite of day but the very stuff of existence. Flung into a whirlwind of pleasure, pretty debutantes flew from one city to another, floating from the first peppery sip at cocktail hour to the last drink in a nightclub. Clad in satin, cigarette in hand, they waited for love, listening to songs by Cole Porter and the heart-rending wail of Benny Goodman's clarinet. The music seemed made for them, as did the summer nights, when champagne-tinted moonlight cast shadows into which they could stray with foolish young men.

The carousel whirled faster, then shuddered to a stop. Girls had at most three seasons to find a companion for the rest of their days. The stakes were high. Marriage was the passport to independence, the only serious career available. Beneath many debutantes' cool exteriors flowed intense undercurrents of anxiety.

Susan Mary knew the game and accepted the rules. She was not quite sure what she wanted and did not have a plan, just a few dreams. She was not as ambitious as Marietta Peabody, though she admired her friend's blond sex appeal, patrician allure, and the bold declaration that she was looking for a man with fortune and power. Less pleasure-bent as well, Susan Mary hoped to find some use for her quick mind and intelligence. Although her character and ideas had not pushed her to rebel or to relinquish the privilege and security of her upbringing, she could not imagine a future limited to a husband, a nursery full of children, a nice garden, and bridge parties, even if the china was from Sèvres and the dresses came from Paris. It may have been her genes, or the result of her childhood abroad: she was fascinated by the outside world. She had a strong interest in history and a taste for current events.

Her entry onto the scene went smoothly. Life had dealt her several winning cards, including her name and her position, and she had improved the state of her hand by acquiring a social ease that was entirely her own creation. She had fought down timidity, although the death of her father in October 1933, leaving her with a mother who showed little affection, had not helped. Spurred on by a romantic desire to see and conquer the world, she had forced herself to be outgoing, to gain poise and composure. Her beauty developed, hesitantly at first, but as she lost weight, her features grew more refined. She wore her smooth, dark hair parted on the side or in the middle, in gentle, shoulder-length waves; with a lock on her forehead, prettiness eluded her. She was always carefully dressed, and although she rarely laughed, her serious and inquisitive gaze added to her charm.

Unlike some girls who were interested only in chasing men, Susan Mary also cultivated friendships with other women. There was Marietta, whose grandfather, the Reverend Endicott Peabody, had founded the famous Groton School, thus involuntarily contributing to his granddaughter's popularity and assuring her an unending flow of young men from girlhood onward; Pauline Louise du Pont, the amusing heiress of the fabulously wealthy family that would commercialize the first nylon stockings in 1939; gentle, sweet Elise Duggan, who wrote short stories in secret and attracted men without even trying; and Dottie Robinson, who kept her homes open to guests both in New York and at Henderson House, a crenellated white mansion built in homage to her family's Scottish origins. In the company of these young women, Soozle (as Susan Mary was known to her friends) played bridge, golf, and tennis, went shopping, and had her hair and nails done. In 1938, she spent more time in New York than in Washington, volunteering at the YWCA and taking classes at Barnard, nothing too demanding. Serious business began at the end of the afternoon. The young men Susan Mary knew worked hard during the day—times were tough, even for Ivy League graduates—but in the evening, they went about their social pursuits with as much energy as they had put into work. Her friends were Jimmy Byrne and William Breese, who were both studying diplomacy in Washington; Curtis Prout, a medical student; and the extremely handsome Stewart Rauch, an assistant to a Democratic senator from Virginia.

Weekends were spent in elegant houses on Long Island or in Avon, Connecticut, where the Alsop clan gathered. Susan Mary got along well with the family's three sons, who had lived and breathed politics since childhood. Their grandmother was Theodore Roosevelt's sister, and their mother, Corinne, was first cousin to Eleanor Roosevelt, who had married her own distant cousin Franklin, the current president. Corinne was an active member of the Republican Party and had been elected to the Connecticut House of Representatives in 1924, four years after American women had won the right to vote. She detested the politics of her cousin in the White House, but she remained proud of her Roosevelt connections.

Susan Mary most admired Joe, the eldest Alsop son. He had gone to Washington as a matter of course, and begun a brilliant career as a political reporter. Still, she had more fun with his younger brothers. Corinne would have liked her to marry Stewart, who had not done much since leaving Yale, but it was John, the youngest son, who wrote Susan Mary teasing letters reproaching her for behaving like a disdainful Scarlett O'Hara.

Several times a year, Susan Mary would take the night express train to Bar Harbor. The following morning, she woke up to the ocean, dotted with white sails. She would give her mother a kiss and hurry off to the club, where the waiters set up tables and umbrellas on the lawn at noon. Ladies sipped aperitifs while young, tanned bodies lay around the pool below, supplying gossip for their elders. Protected from the sun by small round sunglasses and folded newspapers over their heads, Susan Mary and Marietta would try again and again to talk their friend Bill Blair out of his Republican and isolationist opinions. Vibrant, eloquent, the two girls looked lovely, Susan Mary very slim and her friend so spectacular in a black two-piece bathing suit that she turned the heads of all the men who had not gone sailing. Picnics were organized, as were golf tournaments, boat outings, or cocktails at the Peabodys' house in Northeast Harbor. Friends came up from Boston and New York and immediately fell into the happy indolence of youth. On Saturdays, there were dances at the club and everybody smoked too much. Later in life, Susan Mary would recall impossibly beautiful summers when in fact the fog often covered the mountains and turned the ocean gray.

In 1939, Susan Mary decided to earn money with her writing. She moved in with her uncle Elliot Cross, the husband of her mother's sister, dear Aunt Martha. One of Susan Mary's friends, Barbara Cushing, who would later marry CBS founder William S. Paley, had been hired by *Vogue* as a fashion editor because she was photogenic and had great beauty, style, and connections.

Barbara, whom most people knew as Babe, helped Susan Mary write an enthusiastic article on the glorious future that was in store for open-toed shoes, after which *Vogue* offered her a job as a receptionist for twenty-six dollars a week.

During the summer of 1939, the New York World's Fair gave people a chance to admire the city's most recent architectural marvels like the Empire State Building and Rockefeller Center. Babe and Susan Mary posed for a *Vogue* photo shoot in evening gowns, hanging in the air from invisible harnesses with the fair as background. It was a well-paid gig for amateur trapeze artists.

But things got even better. One evening that same summer, while Marietta was away, her fiancé, Desmond FitzGerald, invited Susan Mary to dinner at the Maisonnette Russe, a fashionable restaurant in the St. Regis Hotel. At the end of the meal, he signaled to an old Harvard buddy to join them. In a flash, any feelings Susan Mary might have had for other men vanished like rabbits scattering at the blast of a shotgun. Her eyes lit up as they met the stranger's gaze.

Bill Patten

Everybody loved Bill, and not just out of pity. Asthmatic since childhood, Bill had been pampered by his parents, William and Anna Patten, both Bostonians from good families—and in Anna's case, rich. When he was fourteen, Bill's parents sent him to Groton, where he met Joe Alsop, who was born a year after him, in 1910. Neither boy corresponded to the athletic ideal espoused by the school's venerated British models: Bill was sickly and Joe much too fat. Still, Groton's severe teachers and even

Reverend Peabody took a liking to young Bill Patten. It was the same story at Harvard. Whereas Joe, sweaty and short of breath, earned his stripes through clownery, storytelling, unabashed snobbery, and brilliant intelligence, Bill just smiled the winning smile that made two deep dimples appear at the corners of his mouth. Though Harvard claimed to have a more democratic and intellectual atmosphere than other universities, social success was still considered as important as academic grades, and this was measured by admittance into the elite final clubs. Both Bill and Joe were admitted to the Porcellian Club, Harvard's most selective, making them equals to former member Theodore Roosevelt and giving them a slight advantage over Franklin, whom the Porcellian had passed over.

By the time Bill met Susan Mary he was almost thirty. He had a group of close friends, and was as asthmatic as ever. Professionally speaking, he worked for a Boston brokerage firm and had done nothing worthy of reproach, but he did not have much in the way of a future. Choices made with personal happiness in mind rarely seem reasonable, and quite a few people pointed out the drawbacks of marrying Bill, which Susan Mary had immediately wanted to do. Well-wishers told her she was too young, and that Bill was too sick. Charles Francis Adams, a friend of Bill's from Harvard, took her aside at a party and explained that Bill had to marry for money because his poor health forbade him from earning it. This line of reasoning hardly shocked Susan Mary. She was aware of the laws of matrimony but she was not going to let them stop her. She could allow for the fact that Bill ought to be looking for an heiress, but if that was not his intention, she was not going to stand aside. She saw no reason to give up the things about Bill that made her happy: his good humor, courage, kindness, and the concern he showed for her. She felt as though Bill would always let her pass through a doorway first, that he would always be on her side in times of conflict. He would not be a guide or a tutor, but a dear and tender friend. She had considered the match from every angle, and had found that there was more complexity to Bill than his gentle temperament initially let on. As far as his health was concerned, she thought she could cure him.

The mothers made their inspections. Susan Mary was invited to meet the formidable Anna at her house in Lenox, Massachusetts. (Anna had remarried a bishop, Monsignor Davies, after William Patten's death in 1927.) In turn, Susan Jay came to New York to meet her daughter's beau. Having cared for her own husband during his asthma attacks, she had doubts about Bill's possible recovery, but Susan Mary and Bill were determined to marry and the rest of the family stood behind them. The date was set for October.

Marietta's wedding to Desmond FitzGerald in Northeast Harbor gave Bill and Susan Mary a chance to rehearse, for they were both in the bridal procession. Bill was not at his best, thin and stiff in his jacket, looking like an elegant scarecrow with hollow cheeks and a set smile. His fiancée wore a sea-green dress in draped jersey with a high collar and nasturtiums in her hair that made her look prim and silly. There were torrential rains and the guests spent the entire evening huddled around the radio listening to the news. The German army had invaded Poland the previous day.

A few weeks later, on October 28, 1939, in the little white chapel on his Long Island estate, Susan Mary's uncle, Delancey

Jay, led her down the aisle. She and Bill had lost little time, for they knew, like Marietta and Desmond and indeed their entire generation, that war was looming. They needed to hurry if they wanted to live and love before it began.

A Date Which Will Live in Infamy

For their honeymoon in November 1939, the Pattens rented a cottage at Cuernavaca, near Mexico City. It was covered with balconies and had a pool, three bedrooms, and a cascading series of five different gardens. From the sitting room, there was a view of the violet hills and snow-capped volcanoes in the distance. Susan Mary played at being the lady of the house, and discussed menus with the cook, who patiently endured her dictionary Spanish and served exquisite meals. Bill went riding, played golf, and shot pigeons. Susan Mary could hear his breathing improve. The little city of Cuernavaca, with its pink houses and tile roofs, was known for having a warm and gentle climate. On weekends, it filled up with foreigners and Mexicans leaving the capital to get some fresh air. Susan Mary enjoyed having guests for dinner and wrote her mother candid and lighthearted letters almost daily. She was proud to get by so well on her own. Amid the serenity of those few months in Mexico, she still tried to find out as much as she could about the developing war, which she found very strange indeed.

After the shock of Hitler's brutal attack on Poland, the American people were convinced that he could not face down the British naval blockade and France's impenetrable Maginot Line. It was also thought that the difference between German and

Russian railroad gauges would preclude the continuation of the German campaign on the Eastern Front. The April 1940 invasion of Denmark and Norway, followed by that of the Netherlands, Belgium, and France the following month, soon cast aside these illusions. Congress authorized the draft of all men between the ages of twenty-one and thirty-five, and President Roosevelt sent fifty destroyers to the British. Although the vast majority of Americans hoped for an Allied victory and praised England's courage in the air battle with Germany that had begun in August 1940, they were not ready to get involved. A significant number of politicians were even actively campaigning against American intervention, together with influential groups, such as the America First Committee, whose supporters included Charles A. Lindbergh, an admirer of the Luftwaffe, who thought Great Britain should make peace with the Axis powers. Roosevelt and his Republican adversary, Wendell Willkie, were careful about their statements on the European war during the presidential campaign in the fall of 1940. They both declared their support of Great Britain by all means except armed intervention, promising to keep the United States out of the war.

American involvement grew during 1941 with the passing of the Lend-Lease Act, placing seven billion dollars at the disposition of the British, followed by the proclamation of the Atlantic Charter between Roosevelt and Churchill. But it was the Japanese attack on the naval base at Pearl Harbor on the morning of December 7, 1941, that finally led Roosevelt to request and obtain the declaration of war on Japan from a nearly unanimous Congress. In turn, Germany and Italy declared war on the United States on December 11. The massive American war machine quickly rolled into motion and nearly ten million men were called up, trained, and sent into combat.

Bill's asthma made him a category 4F, which meant he was unfit for military service. He refused to move to Arizona as his doctors had recommended, and looked for a way to earn a little money so as to be less dependent on his mother. He also wanted to serve his nation out of uniform. First, he worked on the presidential campaign for the Republican candidate, Willkie, who was considered more supportive of the Allies; then, after Roosevelt's victory over Willkie, he found a job organizing civil defense for the city of Boston. In November 1942, thanks to his mother-in-law, he was hired by the State Department in the service of Sumner Welles, the undersecretary of state to Cordell Hull and a former colleague of Peter Jay's. The Pattens left Boston for Washington. Susan Mary was glad to return to the capital and relieved that Bill could finally stop feeling useless and comparing himself unfavorably to his enlisted friends. Joe Alsop was a prisoner of war in a Japanese camp in Hong Kong, Charles Adams was in the marines, and Desmond FitzGerald had been drafted as a simple soldier.

In November 1944, the State Department offered Bill a job as an economic analyst for the foreign service with a salary of thirty-eight hundred dollars a year. His first assignment was to the American Embassy in Paris.

Paris

A Voyage to Paradise

> *The ticket cost a hundred and fifty dollars, very cheap for a voyage to paradise.*[1]
>
> —Susan Mary Alsop, *To Marietta from Paris*

Bill left for Paris in January 1945, and Susan Mary went to stay with her mother in Georgetown while she waited for clearance to join her husband, no simple matter in wartime. Their time apart dragged on. Susan Mary was eager to begin her new life as a diplomat's wife in a city where both her father and grandfather had once served America's interests. She was also looking forward to a greater degree of financial and psychological autonomy. Mrs. Jay always seemed to disapprove of her daughter's decisions, and her generosity inevitably came with tiresome lectures about thrifty housekeeping. For Susan Mary, Paris was a promise of independence and peace, a haven far from her meddling mother, a link with the family's past.

The itinerary for the journey eventually arrived, indicating a date, time, and location that had to be kept secret until the last minute. At ten in the evening on March 31, 1945, a friend dropped her off on a pier in New York. She boarded the long military ship with two suitcases, a handbag, a typewriter, a hatbox, and a few orchids. The next morning, her ship joined twenty others to form a convoy on the high seas under the protective escort of destroyers and Catalina seaplanes. Rules were strict. Passengers had to drink their sherry out of toothbrush mugs, dine at five in the afternoon, and wear life jackets all the time. Still, the officers were perfect gentlemen, and Susan Mary rather enjoyed obeying them, and disobeying them too. One night, she stepped out of her cabin when the convoy was under fire from one of the last German attacks and was soundly reprimanded.

Twelve days later, Susan Mary disembarked at Southampton and took the train to London, where she discovered the grim reality of war. Everywhere she turned there were houses that had been blown to bits, gutted buildings, barbed wire, and craters full of black water. Squadrons of bombers continually flew overhead on the way to Germany. The people were poorly dressed and underfed, but kept smiling in the knowledge that victory was near; restaurants, bars, and nightclubs were full of officers and pretty women. Susan Mary was delighted to see her English friends after so long and excited at the thought of being reunited with Bill. Flattered by the attention she received from several men in uniform, she fell under the spell of London's giddy atmosphere.

This happiness was somewhat dampened by the news of Roosevelt's death. On the few occasions she had visited the White House at the invitation of young Franklin Jr. and Ethel du Pont,

Susan Mary had not been impressed by the late president. She had always hoped, in vain, to hear interesting revelations from the statesman who had stood up to Wall Street and fascism. One evening, in December 1942, shortly after the beginning of the Allied Operation Torch in North Africa, Roosevelt began talking about the French admiral Darlan while preparing martinis. He said that he agreed with Eisenhower: Darlan was a rascal, albeit a useful one. This promising opening was dropped when they were called to the dinner table. Roosevelt withdrew behind a humorous, impenetrable façade and told dull stories about sailing, his passion. The Pattens went home disappointed. But when Susan Mary found herself sitting on a bench in St. James's Park on the morning of April 13, she felt very far from home and mourned the death of her president. Nobody knew much about Harry Truman, the man who would take his place.

Finally, on April 17, Susan Mary left London for Paris. After twenty-two hours of continuous travel, she arrived at the Gare du Nord at six in the morning. Bill was waiting for her on the platform, and springtime in Paris was waiting outside.

Another Climate

> *I went away,*
> *Thousands of miles away, to another climate,*
> *To another language, other standards of behavior . . .*
>
> —T. S. Eliot, *The Elder Statesman*

Of the thirty thousand Americans who lived in Paris before the war, five thousand had stayed throughout the Occupation against the advice of their ambassador, William Bullitt. In August 1944, the Liberation brought a wave of new arrivals. Journalists and spies came first, with diplomats and commanding forces of the Allied armies right behind them. Soon, even businessmen started to return. By the spring of 1945, Yankee Paris was back in full swing, with its army post exchange stores and embassy receptions. If she had wanted, Susan Mary could have spent her time with Americans, but that was not the way she saw things. She set herself three goals: she would help Bill as well as she could in his new job (making friends with bankers and important figures in the finance ministry and the Bank of France), she would try to understand the country, and she would try to meet French people. To reach these goals, she had a passable mastery of the language, two letters of introduction, and a pretty house at 21, square du Bois de Boulogne on the avenue Foch that belonged to her mother's Aldrich cousins.

Susan Mary already knew the house where she had reluctantly spent several childhood vacations. When she began her inspection on the morning of her arrival, it seemed as if nothing had changed, although the Germans had occupied the premises until the Liberation. Accompanied by the cook, Madame Vallet, she walked through the two sitting rooms and the dining room decorated with lilacs from the garden before heading upstairs to the smaller salon and the bedrooms. The Aubusson carpets still covered the floor, the Guardi paintings had not been damaged, and the silver, china, and glassware were all in place. Susan Mary congratulated Madame Vallet, who took a suitably demure air. What was more, it appeared they were in luck: the Germans had left four tons of coal behind, enough for them to have hot water every other day.

After the inspection, the two women came to the pressing subject of food. Almost a year after the Liberation, finding something to eat was still the city's principal obsession. Susan Mary did not eat much, but there were the appetites of Bill and their future guests to consider. Bread, potatoes, and a few pathetic-looking vegetables could be bought with ration cards, but the rest—the essentials—would come from the larders of the American army. When Madame Vallet pointed out that there were other options, Susan Mary told her that Bill had said the black market was off-limits. Nonsense, insisted Madame Vallet, it was impossible to run a house without resorting to such measures, and besides, what Bill didn't know wouldn't hurt him. Susan Mary did not dare argue.[2]

The next day, the army supplies arrived in huge twelve-pound cans: bacon, vegetables, fruit, powdered eggs, milk, and chocolate. Once a week they got a roast or a piece of poultry. Everything was kept under lock and key. Susan Mary later realized how privileged she was when she saw the watery soups and creamless cream served in Paris's finest houses. Her American supplies also made it easy to hire an excellent maid. "Madame will of course have American army provisions?," the agency's director had asked hopefully.

With housekeeping problems taken care of, Susan Mary turned to her duties as a diplomat's wife. Custom had it that a new arrival left her calling card at the homes of her husband's colleagues. Susan Mary was summoned one morning by a woman whose husband was the embassy's political adviser. Her hostess received her in bed with a glass of bourbon already in hand, and warned that Bill's job was too unimportant for Susan Mary to hope to meet the ambassador's wife. Ever polite, Susan Mary listened in silence, sent off a few letters to Washington, and soon found herself dining with the American ambassador, Jefferson Caffery.

V-E Day

Susan Mary's other urgent concern was finding work, something she managed easily. Many American soldiers spent their leave in Paris, so the American Red Cross had set up clubs that housed up to ten thousand men. The oldest among them, which had been functioning since September 1944, was called the Rainbow Corner and was located on the boulevard de la Madeleine. Susan Mary went there three times a week dressed in a khaki uniform and cap. She would ride her bicycle along the avenue Foch, with its blooming chestnut trees, before turning onto the Champs-Élysées. Due to gas shortages, there were few cars in the streets, but the American military policeman who directed traffic at the place de la Concorde always recognized her and stopped what little traffic there was to let her turn into the rue Royale, saying, "Go on, miss, I'll take care of the French."

Assigned to the information office, she was charged with, among other things, tracking down Americans and Frenchmen, both civilian and military, whose friends and families were without news. Sorting papers and checking facts, Susan Mary learned about the war and what human beings are capable of doing to one another. Toward the end of the year, she found herself holding the file of Fritz Colloredo-Mansfeld. One of Bill's best friends, he had signed up for the Royal Air Force in September 1939 and had disappeared over the French coast of the English Channel. She and Bill would later visit his grave in an isolated, windswept field.

On May 8, 1945, Susan Mary listened with her French friends at the Rainbow Corner as General de Gaulle, head of the provisional French government, announced on the radio the end of the war in Europe following the signing of the German Instrument of Surrender in Reims the previous day. Like many of her fellow countrymen, starting with the late Franklin Roosevelt, who suspected that General de Gaulle harbored ambitions that were less than democratic, Susan Mary did not know what to think of de Gaulle and his political future. Still, she regretted that the Allies had waited so long to recognize the provisional French government (which they finally did on October 23, 1944). As de Gaulle's voice pronounced the time-worn words *gloire, honneur,* and *patrie* to praise the Allies and the people of France, she, like the French themselves, responded with emotion.

In the morning the city was relatively calm, but after lunch, crowds filled the Parisian streets. Flying Fortresses soared over the Arc de Triomphe, which was bristling with flags. All the army jeeps were gathered on the Champs-Élysées and had picked up boys and girls on the way; some of them were even standing on the running boards, and all were hollering at the tops of their lungs. The mass of people was even denser on the place de la Concorde in front of the Hôtel Crillon and the Navy Ministry, buildings that, for the past four years, had flown the hideous

German swastikas. A man stepped out onto the balcony of the American Embassy and made the V sign for victory. Because he was bald and in uniform, the people shouted back, thinking he was Eisenhower. In fact, it was Bullitt, the former ambassador, who had turned over the embassy's keys to Paul Reynaud when he left Paris in June 1940.

Suddenly, everything lit up. The Madeleine, the Opera, and the National Assembly shed their solemn stillness and became ephemeral theater sets for a night of festivity. The air was warm. The Republican Guard continued to parade in the rue Royale, a girl seated in the saddle behind every horseman. The "Marseillaise" and old Resistance songs echoed through the streets. The Pattens watched French faces turn heavenward as fireworks burst and dissolved in shimmering wreaths and ribbons that whistled and fell into the Seine.

Susan Mary would never forget those radiant hours when Paris, laying aside worries and weariness, celebrated victory. Yet when she wrote to her mother about the incredible evening, she ended on a wary note: "The peace is certainly going to be so incredibly difficult."[3]

This Magnificent People

Although the Second World War had not killed as many French citizens as World War I had, half a million people, including civilians, had died. The conflict had left the nation battered and seriously weakened. War and pillaging had caused the economy to fall to pieces, with industrial production barely reaching half of what it had been in 1938. Agriculture fared little better.

Bombing raids had knocked out much of the nation's infrastructure, and no bridge was left on the Seine downstream from Paris, or on the Loire downstream from Nevers. The crippled transportation system was accompanied by a coal shortage and rising prices. The French government had to find the means to help its citizens survive (a million people were homeless, and city dwellers faced shortages of food, heating, and electricity), while also rebuilding the country according to the ambitious plans set forth by the Resistance movements that included nationalizations, urban planning, and social programs. On top of this, the government needed to assert its authority and return to a state of normal function. Vichy had discredited the political class and the chaos of the war's end had created de facto leaders who had little desire to step aside and let legal authorities take over. Morally speaking, the state of the French population was not the same as it had been at the end of the First World War, for although huge hopes for national renewal and solidarity had risen with newfound liberty, everyone was aware that the people of France had not stood united during the conflict. The Occupation and the Liberation had stirred up fear and hatred and led to the settling of scores between enemies. In the wake of so much suffering, tension would take a long time to dissipate.

Eager for new experiences, Susan Mary set off to discover Parisian life, on the streets and in drawing rooms, with a Girl Guide's enthusiasm, a reporter's inquiring eye, and the stubbornness of a woman of the world. Curious and untiring, she explored the city on bicycle, observing everything and recounting her adventures in her letters. She described a well-dressed old gentleman hurriedly picking up a cigarette butt she had dropped on the street, and an auction at the Hôtel Drouot where the queens of the black market snapped up furs and jewelry confiscated from collaborators. She also followed French politics as closely as possible, and met several important players, such as Paul Reynaud, the finance minister René Pleven, and Gaston Palewski, one of General de Gaulle's close aides. Beside American newspapers and magazines like the *New York Herald Tribune, Harper's, Time,* and the *New Yorker,* Susan Mary read the French newspapers, which she found well written but ridiculously small—they were printed on one page only, due to paper shortages. She listened to the comments on the municipal elections in May and the legislative elections in October, where the seats were divided in nearly equal thirds among the Communists (which had become France's largest political party), the MRP (a new Christian-Democratic party), and the Socialists. In December, Bill told her about the debate in the National Assembly on the nationalization of banks and credit unions. Susan Mary's concern for France's monetary situation was far from disinterested. She greeted the December 1945 devaluation of the franc with glee because it meant she could finally afford a dress in one of Paris's coveted but expensive boutiques.

Every occasion was an excuse to investigate her French surroundings. She visited Normandy to buy butter and see if the rumors about the farmers' newfound wealth were true. The ministry of former prisoners of war, victims of deportation, and refugees, headed by Henri Frenay, was just across the street from her house, and she watched with a catch in her throat as the trucks arrived from prisoner-of-war camps. Even more striking were the scenes in the Paris metro in the month of May following the liberation of the concentration camps. When a former prisoner boarded, still wearing his striped uniform, the occupants of the entire car rose to their feet to offer their seats. Susan Mary also tried to come to terms with how French people had behaved during the Occupation. A ceremony organized by the British Embassy to decorate members of the Resistance who had helped the English led her to conclude that heroes came from all walks of life, from modest shopkeepers to old families of the Faubourg Saint-Germain. In July, she attended the trial of Marshal Pétain before the High Court of Justice. Day after day, in an overheated courtroom, she listened to the tearful, grandiloquent justifications of the politicians called in to give testimony until she thought she might be sick. Pétain sat in silence and never came to the stand. All in all, she found the trial chaotic and undignified. Like most Americans, she thought the courts were often too lenient toward those who had profited during the Occupation.

Susan Mary was equally interested in international news. She and Bill entertained often in their well-heated, comfortable house because they enjoyed it, but also because Bill's job required them to do so. Their guests were military men, high-placed French civil servants, and Bill's embassy colleagues. They also invited people in charge of the American zone in Germany and officials who went back and forth between Europe and the United States attending the postwar international conferences. Most of the guests were old friends. The diplomats Chip Bohlen, Paul Nitze, and Nicky Nabokov often dropped in. One August evening, Joe Alsop came to dinner, looking dapper in his captain's uniform. He was in Paris with General Chennault, under whom he had served in China.

Susan Mary never knew how many people would be coming to dinner, but she soon began to blossom as a hostess, a role that would later make her famous. She knew how to mix people and ideas, how to lower the lights, and how to spice up conversation with alcohol. She found that well-managed hospitality was not without benefits. Beyond the pleasures of friendship, she liked receiving fresh and reliable news from all over the world, even though it was not always good. It seemed that things were very unstable in Germany. The Americans did not have their zone under control, and the Russian officers were worried at the idea of a new war against their former allies. Susan Mary was concerned by these problems coming so soon after the end of the fighting. She had been horrified by America's use of the atomic bomb and feared that her country would have to play an imperial role in the world. "My instinct is that we are going to be forced into an exertion of global power that we neither desire nor are ready to fulfill," she wrote the day after Christmas.[4]

Instead of keeping a diary or writing articles, Susan Mary recorded her lucid, detailed, and careful analyses in letters to her mother and her friend Marietta FitzGerald. These letters, written almost daily, show astonishing maturity and perspective for such a young woman. She refused to behave like other Americans stationed in Paris who often dealt in stereotypes, saw corruption everywhere, and were convinced that France was falling into anarchy. She thought the naysayers were too quick to believe the figures given in American newspapers about the killing of supposed collaborators by former Resistance fighters. She tried to stay as informed as possible, comparing different sources and passing judgment only as a last resort. She was most interested in what the French themselves had to say, even if she did not hesitate to express her own opinions.

Although she was more of an Anglophile and never automatically defended the French—she felt there were too many military parades and days off from work—Susan Mary pointed out their courage and hospitality. She admired the calm with which they greeted tragic events like the loss of a relative in the camps, and noted their general lack of resentment toward the Allies for the damage caused by bombings. The unfavorable comparisons that many American soldiers stationed in Germany made between the French and the Germans angered her. She disliked the triumphalism of the victors, and thought it unfair to despise the French or expect cowed gratitude from them. Rather, she felt it was both an intellectual and a moral obligation to side with the wounded French nation. When the military governor of Paris decried the barbarian behavior of American troops, she was not far from agreeing with him. This sympathy for France's difficulties was so strong that it often left her feeling discouraged. A few weeks after settling in Paris, she admitted her sadness. "There have been blue moments. The euphoria of arrival wore off. It then struck me that Paris was the most beautiful city I had ever been in but that it was like looking at a Canova death mask. I am sure I am wrong and that the vitality of this magnificent, exasperating, heroic people will return."[5]

French Friendships

Susan Mary's attitude can be explained, at least in part, by the immediate bonds she made with several families that introduced her into Parisian society. Grateful to her friends and responsive to their kindness, she broadly generalized her positive feelings about the French and attributed to all the virtues she had noticed in a few.

Her first letter of introduction took her to the house of a family of well-fed and whiny collaborators to which she did not return. The results of the second letter were another story altogether. She went to the house of Henri and Marie de Noailles, at 52, avenue d'Iéna, with the package of needles, thread, safety pins, chocolate, and instant coffee that their son had entrusted her with in Washington. They invited Susan Mary and Bill to dinner, and the four of them ate in the concierge's apartment, where there was a stove to keep them warm. After dinner, they went into a small, elegant salon, which also had a stove, and talked quietly about the events of the war.

The Pattens and the Noailles saw each other often. The Noailles liked the young, well-educated couple who seemed to be curious about everything French. Susan Mary had read Balzac and knew this was the upper crust, a noble family faithful to the past, but without any dusty, paralyzing nostalgia. Henri de Noailles took Susan Mary under his wing and saw to her artistic and social education, leading her to the few rooms that were open in the Louvre, to auctions, and to antique dealers, all the while explaining the ins and outs of French society.

"You must understand," he told her on one of their walks, "the only reason you've been welcomed here is because everybody was so dreadfully bored for four years. In reality, everything is still very closed off."

"But what can I do?" she asked.

"There's nothing you can do. Well, perhaps there are a few simple rules. A well-prepared *côtelette* will lure anybody. And of course, one attracts a lot of Parisians by giving balls, because they are so stingy with their parties. But you can't hope for anything in exchange."[6]

Susan Mary wondered whether what Henri de Noailles was telling her applied to their relationship, and if she was tolerated only as an exotic distraction. She hoped the friendship was mutual, although, even if it was not, she would have been grateful for his company. In truth, Henri de Noailles found Susan Mary utterly beguiling.

Thanks to the Noailles, the Pattens discovered the aristocratic side of France and the grand country houses. They visited the Noailles' château de Mouchy, where the Germans had poked out the eyes in several family portraits before retreating; the château de Grosbois of the La Tour d'Auvergne family; and the château de l'Orfrasière in the Loire Valley, which belonged to the La Panouse family. Their friends took them to visit country neighbors. Every time they walked into an old château, the cold pounced upon them. One child even asked if it was true that people could take off their coats in American sitting rooms. Nevertheless, the Pattens politely admired everything that was shown to them. There was not a garden, it seemed, that had not been designed by Le Nôtre. In turn, the French admired the Pattens' old Chevrolet, which had just been shipped across the Atlantic.

Susan Mary missed the ladies' luncheons that were an essential ingredient of American social life, but eventually she made friends her own age, like Louise de Rougemont, Marie de Maud'huy, and the ravishing Odette Pol-Roger and her sister,

Jacqueline Vernes. Apart from Alix de Rothschild, nobody had new clothes and the women casually wore the things they had worn for the past five years, envying Susan Mary's American stockings and gloves. Susan Mary liked the formality and good manners of the women she met, their old-fashioned grace, politeness toward the elderly, and sense of family. To her thinking, it was the women who were the country's backbone: young girls who took advantage of the newly relaxed rules to go out dancing in nightclubs, stiff old ladies who dressed in black and devoted themselves to attending receptions and funerals, hearty shopkeepers and talkative concierges. Susan Mary was duly impressed and would have liked to award each of them a prize for endurance and energy.

In December 1945, the windows of the Parisian department stores were filled with animated toys for the first time in five years and children pressed against the glass in wonder. On Christmas Day, the house decorated with holly branches, Susan Mary gave a party in two languages before leaving to dine with the Coopers, the British ambassador and his wife. She was becoming a Cooper household regular.

Affairs of the Heart

The Ambassador and the Madonna

When Winston Churchill named his friend Duff Cooper ambassador to France in the autumn of 1944, he was giving him a coveted gift, fully knowing how disobedient Duff was likely to be. Duff was convinced that Western Europe had to unite to resist the American and Soviet giants, and he felt that the cornerstone of this union should be a Franco-British alliance. He took it upon himself to start forging this bond, even though his government had told him otherwise. In Churchill's opinion, becoming closer to France meant currying the favor of General de Gaulle, an idea that put him on the verge of an apoplectic fit. Foreign secretary Anthony Eden was in favor of strong Franco-British relations, but feared it might anger the Soviets. This lack of support did not worry Duff. It would not be the first time he had held out for what he believed to be right, and if he did not get his way, he would always have Paris, his favorite city, to console him, with the Travellers Club, the bookstores, and the fine restaurants he went to in the company of his many lady friends.

Duff was a man of contradictions. Firmly rooted in a traditional, conservative background, he loved work and study and was faithfully attached to his wife, all of which never stopped him from speaking his mind or seeking pleasure in all forms. His entire life, he always did what he felt was right and what he found enjoyable, even if other people thought or lived differently.

Born in 1890, Duff was the son of a respectable surgeon, Sir Alfred Cooper, and of Lady Agnes Duff, the daughter of one of King William IV's ten legitimized children with the Irish actress Dorothea Jordan. Lady Agnes and Alfred Cooper were married, but polite society found it difficult to overlook the fact that she had been married twice before, even if she managed to settle down after the third marriage. She adored her only son, and had named him Alfred Duff—Alfred after his father and Duff after her maiden name.

Duff (he never used the name Alfred) was educated at Eton and Oxford before beginning his career as a diplomat in 1913, a position he abandoned for a few months during the war. He served bravely in the third battalion of the Grenadier Guards and returned with the Distinguished Service Order and a renewed appetite for life. A talented diplomat, Duff was certain that he would soon become a cabinet member. He possessed the joyful confidence that promises and facilitates success. He had a Regency air about him, and particularly admired two figures from that fascinating period: Charles James Fox, the renowned Whig Party politician, and Talleyrand, whose biography he would later write.

Women, literature, and politics were the three interests that occupied Duff's time in equal proportions. His technique for wooing was to compose sonnets and seal the deal. This heady mix of assertive sensuality and intellectual romanticism worked well, and women were attracted in spite of his unremarkable physique, medium height, and round face. He married Lady Diana Manners, one of the stars of her generation, the youngest daughter of the lovely and artistic Duchess of Rutland. Diana was a beauty herself, blond and pale with the doe-eyed, startled expression of silent-movie actresses. Amusing and determined to have a good time, she surrounded herself with a group of friends who were her bulwark and her battle flag. Her looks, high birth, and wild reputation called for the scandalized admiration of her peers and tabloid readers alike, giving her a visibility she grew accustomed to with no trouble at all. She forced her disapproving parents to agree to her marriage to Duff on June 2, 1919, a union that caught the public's imagination as a fairy-tale match between a princess and a commoner. In fact, the two were drawn together by a bond of mutual understanding. Diana's brilliant exterior hid an intellectual inferiority complex and a tendency toward clinical depression; Duff brought calm and balance to her life and appeased her anxious narcissism more surely than drugs. In return, she was a great help to her husband, providing him with full access to Britain's highest social and political circles. Diana's sense of fun, eccentricity, and social position ensured that Duff would never be bored, and allowed him to escape the provincial respectability and petit bourgeois attitude typical of many politicians and civil servants. Diana always provided an irresistible spectacle, be it her shapely profile beneath enormous straw hats worn at even the most inappropriate occasions or the proud, splendidly theatrical towers of Belvoir Castle. Not least, she proved to be smilingly tolerant of Duff's extramarital adventures, delights that he no more intended to give up than fine port, backgammon, and collecting first editions. She asked only to be kept informed, a request that was not always fulfilled. Thanks to his wife (although at what cost to her own peace, one has to wonder), Duff had the satisfaction of being both a loving husband and a dedicated womanizer.

The only thing missing from their tender, if not sensual, relationship was money. Duff wanted to leave the stifling, shadowy hallways of bureaucracy for the bracing atmosphere of the House of Commons, but getting elected was expensive. Diana took it upon herself to transform her childhood love of costumes and playacting into a career. Her heart-shaped face took light well and her name was already famous. She acted in two silent movies before starring as the Madonna in Max Reinhardt's play *The Miracle;* hands clasped, looking up to heaven, she toured the United States during four long winters. She made enough money to allow her husband to run as a Conservative Party candidate. Duff's career took off after his election in 1924 and he held a number of ministerial posts. Some said his future was as promising as Anthony Eden's, while others wrote him off as a dilettante too easily distracted by women, gambling, and drink. In 1935, the prime minister, Stanley Baldwin, named Duff war secretary. Two years later, he was promoted to First Lord of the Admiralty under Neville Chamberlain, a post Winston Churchill had held before World War I and which came with a yacht and a beautiful residence in London.

It was a welcome nomination, in spite of the serious disagreements over foreign policy and defense that had long divided Cooper and Chamberlain. Duff was convinced that Germany's bellicose attitude required a closer alliance with France, and had tried, in all the posts he had occupied, to accelerate British rearmament and create an expeditionary force for eventual intervention on the Continent. But such an alliance was unpopular among those in Conservative circles who felt France was too weak and vindictive and saw Germany as a shield against the Bolshevik threat. Backed by his cabinet and the political class at large, Chamberlain made economic recovery a priority, believing it would guarantee future social harmony. When evidence of Hitler's ambitions became clearer, Chamberlain thought war could be avoided by coming to an understanding with Europe's dictators. While Duff continued to argue in vain for the reinforcement of Britain's naval capacities, Chamberlain took his policy of appeasement to its limits, signing the Munich Agreement with Hitler and sacrificing Czechoslovakia.

This was too much for Duff, who believed that the agreement was both morally unacceptable and politically dangerous. He could not stand behind a calculation that bought peace at the price of a sovereign state. Out of respect for international law and for Great Britain's honor, he resigned from the government the day after Chamberlain's triumphant return from Munich on October 1, 1938. Although some of his colleagues agreed with him, he was the only one who had the courage to leave his post.

Duff had been close to Churchill from the beginning and he

had to wait for the great man's return to power to resume his career. He would briefly serve as minister of information in 1940 before becoming special envoy to the Far East. Finally, in January 1944, he left for Algiers, where he became the British government's representative to General de Gaulle's French Committee of National Liberation. Working with touchy and distrustful de Gaulle was difficult and required all of Duff's patience and tact. Not without reason, the general interpreted every move as an Anglo-American plot to prevent him from taking power in postwar France. Caught between Churchill and de Gaulle, two quick-tempered giants who had decided from the outset that they would not get along, Duff managed to be respected by both men, and to make himself useful. His reward was the job he had been hoping for: ambassador to Paris.

At the Hôtel de Charost

Diana was not thrilled at the idea of leaving Algiers. Had she been given the choice, she would have preferred to continue living in her pajamas until noon rather than face the responsibilities of an important embassy in a country for which she felt no particular attraction. Moreover, Diana's favorite house was always the one she was about to leave. Still, she could not let Duff down, so, once again, she underwent a transformation and turned herself into an unforgettable ambassadress. The Hôtel de Charost, their new residence on the Faubourg Saint-Honoré, was a vast, peaceful, and elegant house imbued with the spirit of Pauline Bonaparte, who had once filled it with the carefree merriment of her parties. Diana was a worthy successor. Whether a grand reception or an intimate dinner, every event held at the embassy had to be unique. Diana boldly ignored protocol, inviting her friends, mixing guests according to her fancy, and creating seating arrangements that paired off Aragon with Malraux; a comic like Noël Coward with the new prime minister, Clement Attlee; or Daisy Fellowes, reputed to be the most stylish woman on two continents, with the old Communist Marcel Cachin. This easygoing attitude led to criticism, both in Paris and in London. The Coopers, it was said, ought to be more careful about opening the embassy to people whose wartime activities had been less than impeccable. These mutterings went unheeded. Diana obeyed her own laws, and Duff, for his part, refused to blame those who had shown less courage than he had. He had no intention of getting involved in the internal conflicts of the French.

Whatever their reason for wanting to be asked, the guests all agreed that Lady Diana was simply marvelous. She entranced a number of men, from stout British statesman Ernest Bevin, who called her "Luff" and often tried to proposition her, to the last bey of Tunis, with whom she communicated by drawing on the table during an entire dinner. Cocteau immortalized the "pale blue pistol shot of her gaze,"[1] and she dazzled the writer François Mauriac with "her adorable beauty."[2]

Thus, without even trying to compete with other salons (the musical evenings of Marie-Blanche de Polignac, Lise Deharme's mezzanine, Florence Gould's lunches, the meetings of the Académie Française at Edmée de La Rochefoucauld's, cosmopolitan gatherings at Marie-Louise Bousquet's, and artistic ones at the house of Marie-Laure de Noailles), the British Embassy became one of the most sought-after centers of Parisian social life. Although she sometimes felt breathless from so much activity, Diana was happy as long as her husband was pleased.

Susan Mary entered the Coopers' inner circle at the end of 1945. Diana had heard about her and invited her to the embassy with Bill. The beautiful Englishwoman was always surrounded by a bevy of admirers—courtiers, her detractors might have said. Her devoted retinue served and flattered her, treating her like a goddess, although on bad days she felt herself fit for the madhouse. To become part of the clique, one had to be beautiful, amusing, or both, and not too obscure or unconnected. Susan Mary met the requirements. She was pretty enough for the fearsome editor of *Harper's Bazaar*, Carmel Snow, to have her regularly photographed, and so striking that Balenciaga sold her dresses at a special price for her to wear at society affairs as a *mannequin du monde*. She was also fashionable enough to be a regular guest of the Duke and Duchess of Windsor in Paris and Antibes. She could be trusted to make conversation about anything, from politics to gossip, and, unlike other society women, she was truly interested in the future of humanity. She read the morning papers not just to shine in the evening but because she had a genuine hope that peace might last and be even more exciting than war.

Still, Susan Mary was not at ease with her glamorous image. When Carmel Snow's assistants admired photographs of her reclining on a sofa in a low-cut evening gown and said she looked like a painting by David, "*mais très* ladylike," she disagreed, thinking she had an idiotic, frozen expression. She blamed herself for idleness since she had stopped working for the Red Cross and considered her French inadequate—for years she would keep making mistakes on the gender of nouns. The letters she sent home dwelled on supposed failures and brushed aside achievements. She described going to tea at the house of a Frenchman who immediately tried to get her into bed. She fought back like a frightened schoolgirl and fled, instead of withdrawing gracefully. The next day, her coat, hat, and gloves were returned and the rejected party became a close friend. She sighed with relief and noted, "Frenchmen may be wonderful lovers. I wouldn't know. Certainly they are very good thwarted lovers, bearing no rancor."[3]

Another story she told against herself was about the charity ball she organized for war orphans. She had reserved the Pré Catelan, a famous restaurant in the Bois de Boulogne, for May 28, 1946, but nobody was buying tickets. In despair, Susan Mary went one morning to the embassy, begging Diana Cooper for help. Sitting in her bed of red damask, a massive Empire affair with carved bare-breasted Egyptian figures, the ambassadress, who loved acting as fairy godmother, hatched a plan. The next day, she and Susan Mary made the rounds of the couturiers, ordering fabric, reserving masks, and loudly congratulating themselves on their good luck at finding a few things still available so near to the date of an important ball. The rumor spread, the tickets sold like hotcakes, and the fete was saved.

Susan Mary had long learned to hide and overcome her lingering feelings of inadequacy. Even more than Washington, Paris demanded that she camouflage any weakness and refuse to feel sorry for herself. One had to keep in line with the relentless perfection of society life. So Susan Mary played her role at embassy receptions with quiet grace, then went home and

mischievously commented on them with Bill. Small parties were
the best. At the end of the day, the regulars would gather around
the fireplace in the green salon on the second floor and drink
their liquor neat. There was Evelyn Waugh, whose friendship
with Diana was as famous as the fits of rage he sparked off in
Duff; Nancy Mitford, who watched her lover, Gaston Palewski,
flirt with other women while noting the idiosyncrasies of her
fellow guests for her next novel; and, above all, Louise de
Vilmorin, enthroned at Diana's side, gloomy when neglected and
brilliant when everybody was listening to her. One evening,
Susan Mary witnessed her fling a lump of butter to the ceiling
(where it stuck) to bring herself back to the center of attention.
The fiery intensity of Cocteau's monologues scared her a little, but
she thought it charming that Christian Bérard should throw
himself at her feet in mock worship every time he saw her in a
new dress.

Susan Mary was even more interested by the company of
politicians and diplomats. There was no vulgar, personal motive
in her desire to be near power. She liked seeing "history on the
boil," as Nancy Mitford put it, being present in a room where the
fate of the world was being played out. She did not ask to be on
the stage itself; a good place in the audience was more than
enough, one from which she could see everything and be seen.
For years, the British Embassy provided her a seat in the front
row.

Indeed, there was much to be seen in 1946. Even as the peace
treaties that were meant to put an end to the war were being
negotiated, distrust grew among the Soviets, the English, and the
Americans over German war reparations, elections in Eastern

Europe, and the United Nations' regulation of atomic energy. On March 5, Churchill was the first to speak of the iron curtain that had fallen across Europe. Familiar with embassies, Susan Mary got to know the leading players: Ernest Bevin, who had replaced Anthony Eden as British foreign secretary; Churchill, out of office but a frequent visitor; and Vyshinsky and Molotov, the Russian ministers of foreign affairs who represented the Soviet threat. A conference on Asian affairs was held that summer at Fontainebleau; Susan Mary was introduced to, and greatly impressed by, Ho Chi Minh. Usually she behaved beautifully at these events, but one evening in September, she tripped up. Seated between Duff and Cocteau at a dinner, she mentioned the speech that had just been given by the American secretary of state, James Byrnes, concerning the need to rebuild Germany. It was quite the wrong thing to do. Ambassador Cooper held views similar to those of the French and was hostile to the idea of the German state rising anew. He exploded with rage. "Duff Cooper can be frightening," she later concluded.[4]

Still, thanks to Susan Mary, the Pattens had become a fixture in the enchanted life of the Hôtel de Charost.

A Strange Affair

> *I found four letters from Susan Mary awaiting me. It is a strange, imaginative affair.*[5]
>
> —Duff Cooper's diary, May 1, 1947

What does a kiss mean? The final touch to a pleasant evening, a sweet mistake, one drink too many? A trial run, a question asked, a promise given? A bolt of lightning, intense desire and fire in the veins? On February 27, 1947, after a dinner at the British Embassy, Susan Mary Patten kissed Duff Cooper, and the solid foundation of her well-ordered life shifted forever.

She had stopped loving her husband a couple of years earlier, and had taken pains not to let him notice. Gentle, kindly Bill deserved the pretense of conjugal bliss. Too many people, she felt, let the fabric of their marriages unravel out of carelessness or a misguided idea of truthfulness. There was no reason for Bill to catch cold just because she had fallen out of love. He had enough to worry about between his asthma, which had not improved in spite of treatments, and the constant threat of losing his job and being called back to the United States. It was best that he remain under the illusion that their relationship still made sense and had substance. Susan Mary had suffered a miscarriage early in their marriage, and the absence of children already made him very sad—she did not want to add to his grief.

Thus did Susan Mary show remarkable self-control in keeping up the appearance of happiness when the real thing eluded her. She would simply turn away when her husband's eyes sought her own or when his hands ran over her unresisting body.

Life is simple when the heart is at rest; so simple that one almost forgets what love feels like. Susan Mary did not immediately understand the nature of the storm that was stirring inside her. One month after their first kiss, Duff went on vacation to Monte Carlo and Susan Mary began writing him cheerful and affectionate letters with increasing frequency. Bedridden with a severe case of gout, Duff enjoyed her stories: an afternoon at Versailles where she accidentally came across a friend making love behind a bush; an unexpected visit from the pompous and insinuating author André Maurois; a weekend stay with Prince Antoine de Ligne at Belœil Castle in Belgium, where the painting above her bed had fallen off the wall, nearly braining her to death in the middle of the night. Duff wrote back in the same vein. When Susan Mary discovered she was not his only correspondent, she feigned indignation. "How many wretched women in Paris, London and New York do you write those lovely letters to? A good two dozen I should think."[6]

On April 29, she opened her heart to Duff, admitting she had fallen madly in love with him a month before. She did not want to hurt Bill, and she admired Diana more than anybody. "I could no more be jealous of her than of God."[7] She hated cheap romance. Perhaps Duff existed only in her imagination, as he himself had suggested, or perhaps it was the reverse. "Has it not occurred to you that you might also have created me out of your illness and boredom? I am not beautiful, you know, but have only a sort of surface prettiness."[8] She was afraid. She left the decision to him.

For Duff, the whole affair was highly flattering and somewhat disturbing. He was not in love with Susan Mary. He was seldom in love, as a matter of fact. He was straightforward about those things, to the point of bluntness. He took his pleasure as he took champagne, frequently, remorselessly, and without measure. Flings began and ended with a laugh. He did not care for women to stir up his life and he did not want to upset theirs. He obeyed a strict set of rules that had long organized the double lives of the English aristocracy, rules as commonly known as those of cricket: keep away from unmarried girls, make compromises, avoid scandal. But Duff also truly enjoyed a woman's company, and he was artfully versed in converting love into friendship. Nothing had prepared him for an earnest American girl married to a Boston puritan.

In truth, Susan Mary had come into Duff's life at exactly the right moment. Weakened by illness, he was also concerned about his professional future. He had been appointed by Churchill, but Churchill had just been rejected by the British. In spite of Ernest Bevin's friendliness, Duff could not help wondering how long the Labor government would keep him in Paris now that a Franco-British treaty had been signed. Besides, he was sentimentally at leisure. His most recent mistress, Gloria Rubio, had left for Kenya, and since the spring of 1946 he was, much to his relief, only a "confidant and *copain*"⁹ to Louise de Vilmorin. Their very public affair had begun in November 1944, and Louise had lost no time moving into the embassy, using the excuse of a cleverly timed fever. For a long period of time, she reigned over this "strange Hôtel Négresco,"¹⁰ as Cocteau described the embassy, playing with verve the triple role of invalid, official mistress, and best friend to her lover's wife. Indeed, Diana had been as charmed as her husband. It was never clear whether lungs, love, or friendship were keeping Louise in a British bed. Duff's feelings changed, but his protection and affection for witty Louise remained. She translated his books and speeches, wrote poetry in his honor, and admired his verses.

So it happened that there was a modest position to be filled. Susan Mary occupied it with talent, carefully disguising her passion under a light and carefree manner, expecting nothing in return. She walked into adultery as tremulously as a governess into her first job; yet she turned out to be a natural, maneuvering like a seasoned courtesan.

Laughter and Nectarines

> *My dearest, dearest Duff, who should have only laughter and nectarines and Pol Roger 34 served you by gay Polynesian dancing girls . . .*
>
> —Letter from Susan Mary to Duff Cooper, May 21, 1947

On May 13, 1947, Odette Pol-Roger and Susan Mary went to England. Odette had been invited by Churchill, her respectful admirer, and Susan Mary had been invited by Ronnie Tree, an American by birth and fortune who lived in England. He had been elected to the House of Commons and was known for his perfect manners and hospitality. He and his wife, Nancy, had bought and renovated Ditchley Park in Oxfordshire, but were undergoing a separation at the time of Susan Mary's visit. Even by British standards, Ditchley was exceptionally luxurious. Susan Mary, joined by Bill for a few days, slept in the best bedroom, decorated in yellow silk, with views of the deer and the follies in the park. She caught a severe cold and had to stay in bed, where she spent most of her time reading Duff's biographies of Field Marshal Haig and King David. She missed lunch with Churchill at Chartwell, but after Bill's departure, she felt well enough to visit Blenheim Palace, see *The Tempest* in Stratford-upon-Avon, and lunch in Oxford with her philosopher friend Isaiah Berlin, whom she had met in Washington and who would soon come to Paris to work on setting up the Marshall Plan.

Shakespeare, the rolling countryside, charming towns named Chipping Norton, Stow-on-the-Wold, and Bourton-on-the-Water—everything in England reminded her of Duff. She had always preferred lords to cowboys, and the ones she met—Ismay and Salisbury—were old friends of the man she could not stop thinking about. In spite of her fever, Susan Mary was a delightful houseguest, talking politics in the drawing room and listening to Ronnie sing the praises of her old friend Marietta FitzGerald, with whom he had fallen in love—they would get married in July. But when she received a letter from Duff, she would impolitely fly off to her bedroom. "Goodnight Lady Moore, goodnight Lady Beatty, Jakie Astor, Sir Richard, Odette, goodnight, goodnight you pack of fools, I am madly in love in the month of May and I have a letter from my lover."[11] She and Duff probably became lovers on May 30 at the Dorchester Hotel, where Duff always stayed when he was in London. "There was a large moon," he wrote in his diary.[12]

Their relationship soon fell into a pattern. Susan Mary and Duff saw each other often during the week, at the embassy or at the houses of mutual friends, a cosmopolitan set that included the Cabrols, who were close to the Windsors; Denise Bourdet, the wife of playwright Edouard Bourdet; Charlie de Beistegui; rich Mrs. Corrigan; and Mogens Tvede and his wife, Dolly Radziwill. On weekends, the Pattens went to Senlis, a country town near Paris, to a pretty house that their American friends the Carters rented to them. From outside, they could see the towers of the Senlis cathedral. Wild strawberries grew in the vegetable garden, and the forest of Chantilly was not far away.

This rural retreat was conveniently located near the château de

Saint-Firmin, which the Coopers rented from the Institut de France. In this light-flooded house with pale-gray rooms, plaster bas-reliefs, and grotesques, Diana became a pastoral Marie Antoinette, pulling ideas for parties out of her hat while John Julius, the Coopers' beloved son, whom Susan Mary dearly liked, played the guitar. The two couples went back and forth, having bridge and tennis at one house, picnics and cocktails at the other. Duff met the Americans who came to visit the Pattens, such as John Alsop and his wife, Gussie; Susan Mary's cousin Charlie Whitehouse; her aunt Aldrich; and the severe mother-in-laws, Mrs. Jay and Mrs. Davies. In Saint-Firmin, Susan Mary saw Churchill and Bevin again. With Bevin she chatted about the Marshall Plan, the importance of which the British statesman had recognized at once. Churchill, on the other hand, insisted on talking with Susan Mary in his incomprehensible but fluent French, something he did when in a good mood. Duff admired the young woman's savoir faire. "Her great charm is her admiration for intelligence and her enthusiasm."[13]

Bill gladly followed his wife into this social whirlwind and got along well with the Coopers. It was not clear whether he knew that their quartet was hiding a duet, but Susan Mary was convinced he did not. At any rate, Bill never showed any sign of torment or bother, just real satisfaction at his wife's obvious happiness.

This was one of the most glorious summers of Susan Mary's life. A sparkling creature seemed to have replaced respectable Mrs. Patten. She wore New Look gowns that Christian Dior lent and even gave her because they flattered her slender waist and handsome bust. "Madame, it does me good to see so much *joie de vivre*," the maître d'hôtel at Maxim's exclaimed one evening after she had stumbled and fallen into his arms. Knowing herself to be loved by Duff, she took to flirting with other men out of pure amusement. For the first time in her life, she stopped equaling happiness with virtue. She was convinced that the only two friends she had confided in about her affair (Odette Pol-Roger and Loelia, the Duchess of Westminster) would keep her secret. She felt protected by her reputation as a modest, even prudish woman. Still, caution was necessary. When her friend Pam Berry, who held a political salon in London, asked her to lunch with Loelia and Ann Rothermere, the future wife of author Ian Fleming, she flatly turned down the invitation, fearing she would be drawn onto dangerous ground by these experts in extracting personal confessions. "I felt slightly like the President of Estonia being asked by Stalin, Vichinsky, and Molotov for a cosy cup of tea to discuss border problems," she wrote to Duff.[14]

Susan Mary stopped worrying about Diana because she had come to understand the unusual and unbreakable relationship that united the Coopers. Her own jealousy remained, but she was determined to keep it in check. "You are one of those people who like to love three or four people at the same time for different reasons and in different ways and that is OK."[15] Happily for her, Duff was an expert in keeping his affairs separate and liked the thrill of multiple clandestine relationships. Susan Mary's self-proclaimed tolerance was never put to the test.

She and Duff saw each other often, but they were seldom alone. As ambassador, Duff had a considerable entourage and little time to himself. He was always surrounded by colleagues and secretaries. A tête-à-tête, like the lunch in Belle Époque style they had in Chennevières on the banks of the Marne on July 16, was a rare occasion. Most of their communication was limited to letters and the telephone. Susan Mary wrote ceaselessly, often in pencil from bed. Her letters were tender and witty, recounting stories from her daily life, passing on gossip and asking for advice on books. She resisted the temptation to slip into introspection and feverish declarations of love, but when she could not take it any longer, she would turn to quotes—"*Ce soir je t'aime trop pour te parler d'amour*"[16]—or poke fun at her own ardor. "It would no doubt be more *convenable* if I could feel platonic about you darling ('Young American woman hero-worships Great Author and Ambassador' sort of thing) but nothing about you arouses the platonic in me."[17]

How could Duff resist the charms of this newcomer to his life, who entertained and flattered him, asking innocently, "Is there a life of you?,"[18] revealing her intelligence with flirtation and her charm through solemnity. Susan Mary learned and loved, a tearless and guilt-free Madame de Tourvel.

In the autumn of 1947, Duff went on holiday to San Vigilio on Lake Garda in Italy. On September 15, Susan Mary wrote to him, "My pleasant spoiled life has become a mechanical series of days to be got through somehow till I see you again." On September 17: "Even my toes feel excited"; and on the same day: "My life has reduced itself to the simple fundamentals of seeing you as much as possible and keeping Bill happy." She continued writing from London on September 28: "What I really want is to lie in your arms again and not think at all." September 30: "Darling, darling will I really see you in three days?" On October 3, they were reunited at Ditchley, now the home of the newly wedded Ronnie and Marietta Tree. Bill was at a London clinic treating his asthma. "The arrangement of the rooms was admirable," wrote Duff in his diary, "Susan Mary and I, in the pink and blue bedrooms respectively, had practically a flat to ourselves. I enjoyed every minute of the day and most of the night."[19] Susan Mary would later write of "the perfect happiness of those two days and three nights at Ditchley."[20]

None of this kept Duff from making the most of an opportunity. When he learned that Susan Mary was in bed with a cold she had caught from him at Ditchley, he chuckled to himself that the cold had probably come from a girl to whom he had made love one night outdoors. Shortly afterward, he turned down a lunch invitation from Susan Mary, pretending he had an important business meeting. In fact, he had a lunch date with two women. One was a former mistress, and he hoped to add the second to his list of conquests. When he went to pick her up, he was horrified to discover she lived next door to the Pattens. "It was unlucky but not, as far as I am aware, discovered."[21] Two days later, the woman was in his bed.

A Farewell Party

Storm clouds gathered over Paris during the winter of 1947. The disastrous economic climate was causing a wave of strikes. To make things worse, the cold war had begun. In early 1947, the American administration had come to the conclusion that the threat of Soviet expansion in Europe had to be counterbalanced through financial aid to its allies. Harry Truman's speech on March 12, 1947, followed by that of Secretary of State George

Marshall at Harvard on June 5, introduced the plan that would use dollars to fight Communism. Financial aid was refused by the U.S.S.R., which forced Poland, Czechoslovakia, and Yugoslavia to do the same. The Marshall Plan would cause the final rupture between the United States and the U.S.S.R.

France chose sides. The government needed American aid to pursue the modernization plans begun by Jean Monnet in order to improve the daily life of the population. But while waiting for aid, the country's economy fell deeper into crisis. In November, three million workers went on strike to protest against rising prices and stagnant wages. Public buildings were taken by assault, arms factories occupied, telegraph lines cut, and rail lines sabotaged. Electricity was cut off and mail delivery was interrupted. The Communist Party, which had no cabinet ministers since their dismissal by Paul Ramadier in May, decided to oppose the government and play on national fears, proclaiming that the Marshall Plan was aimed at rebuilding Germany so that it could better fight Russia in the forthcoming war. At the height of the violence and provocations, the CGT, one of France's major trade unions, unexpectedly called off the strike on December 9. In Le Havre, the dockworkers returned to their jobs just in time to receive the first Marshall Plan shipments arriving from America.

During those troubled months, the American ambassador, Jefferson Caffery, kept the State Department informed of the situation, which was, according to his French colleagues, close to insurrection. As usual, Susan Mary tried to keep a balanced view. Although she fumed about France being "a nation of *frondeurs*,"[22] she saw the strikes as coming from a determined minority rather

than reflecting, as claimed, popular will. She also knew that
wages were too low and that many of the workers' demands were
justified. She was nevertheless extremely relieved when the
flare-up came to an end. It meant the Coopers' farewell ball could
take place. Duff had been told in September that his time was up,
and he had scheduled the ball for December 10.

Many people came from England to see the embassy lit by
candlelight one last time and to find out whether Parisian women
were really better dressed than their English counterparts. To
Susan Mary's disappointment, the Trees did not come: Ronnie
was afraid of riots and Marietta did not think it fitting to dance
while Paris burned, displaying a political conscience that
displeased her husband's friends. Churchill, however, did not
want to miss the opportunity of seeing his dear Odette Pol-Roger
and of being acclaimed by the crowds gathered in front of the
embassy. The French government was represented by René Mayer,
Jules Moch, and Robert Schuman, the new president of the
French council of ministers, who Susan Mary thought had the
handsome, sensitive expression of an intellectual. The Empire
china had been brought out, the men wore their decorations, and
the women their most beautiful gowns: blue satin and tulle for
Diana, black velvet from Grès for Nancy Mitford, and for Susan
Mary, a mauve satin and ivory grosgrain creation that Elsa
Schiaparelli had insisted on making. She had a wonderful time
and danced until five in the morning.

It was closing time in the embassy gardens. Duff and Susan
Mary lunched together at Lapérouse on December 15. The final
farewell was played out in the Gare du Nord late in the morning
of December 18. It was quite a dramatic scene. Louise de Vilmorin

hurried toward the train as though she might throw herself on the tracks, declaring she couldn't live without the Coopers and that she was leaving for England with them. (This, in fact, had been planned long ago. Her luggage was already on the train.) The train pulled away and those left behind on the platform went off to rest after having had a delicious cry. Susan Mary turned homeward, heartbroken.

V

The Age of Serenity

An American Boy

The date was admirably chosen for the birth of an Ameri-can boy.[1]

—Duff Cooper's diary, July 4, 1948

"You see, Doctor," said Susan Mary, slipping back into her skirt, "for weeks now my clothes have become too tight." She pulled up the zipper. "And to think my friends all say I'm too thin." The doctor she had been seeing since the previous winter for liver problems gave her a strange look and asked her to undress again. She left with the address of a gynecologist she was to consult as soon as possible. When the verdict finally came in, it turned out she was four months pregnant.

"Susan Mary told me rather solemnly today that she is going to have a baby and that it will probably arrive at the beginning of July. She has been married nine years but this is her first," wrote Duff in his diary on February 8, 1948.[2] What did Susan Mary tell her lover that evening? Duff had returned to France a few weeks after his departure and had set up house between the château de Saint-Firmin and a little Parisian pied-à-terre at 69, rue de Lille. Had she reminded him of the nights they had spent together in the blue and pink apartment at Ditchley four months before? Did she sit on his knees, as she usually did, with her head resting on his shoulder, or had she remained standing, stiffened by emotion and stripped, for once, of the desire to please? "Susan Mary told me rather solemnly . . ." With these few offhand words, Duff Cooper made it clear that the expected baby was Susan Mary's business and did not involve him in the least. He would never show any feeling, simply worrying about Susan Mary's health as a friend is concerned about an expectant mother.

Bill expressed only joy and Susan Mary convinced herself it was all for the best.

The following months went by very quietly. The noise of the city barely penetrated the peace of the Patten household. Susan Mary took a break from the embassies and cocktail parties and no longer felt responsible for the international situation, dire though it was. At the end of February, a coup in Prague, approved of by the French Communist Party, raised the fear of a Soviet invasion, with tanks rolling all the way to Paris. Nancy Mitford admitted her panic in a letter to her favorite correspondent, Evelyn Waugh. "I wake up in the night sometimes in a cold sweat. Thank goodness for having no children, I can take a pill & say goodbye. Oh dear, I'm in a state. You should see the states of all my friends here—bags packed and sandwiches cut."[3] Serious and intellectual Susan Mary spent her time going over the layette her mother had sent from Washington. Wearing pretty hand-me-down maternity clothes given by Babe Paley (French shops sold only shapeless smocks), she took walks in the Bois de Boulogne with her boxer, Charlus, before going home and lying on the sofa to dream about her baby. She already had a fairly precise idea of who it would look like.

William Samuel Patten Jr. was born in the maternity ward of the American Hospital in Neuilly on July 4, 1948. Bill was at his wife's side, as well as Mrs. Jay, who, unable to find a taxi, had convinced a car passing on the Champs-Élysées to take her to Neuilly for a pack of American cigarettes. The next day, Susan Mary, who had given birth under anesthesia, felt sufficiently clear-headed to receive a visit from Diana Cooper, who brought her flowers, and to write to Marietta Tree. She also wrote a long letter in answer to the one she had received from Duff. "I am glad that Diana did not have time to see Billy as although in a week or so he will look like any other baby, newborn ones are often a ludicrous caricature of what they will look like when they are much older. If Diana had happened to catch him feeling bored, as when he is woken up to be checked at by his grandmother, the only possible remark she could have made would have been that he was sitting between Mme Bidault and Mme Moch and looked it. I do wish I could draw to show you. At first I was frightened but it is OK."[4] "A lovely, very indiscreet letter," noted Duff in his diary.[5] He in turn went to the hospital on July 13 and found the young mother "very pretty and in high spirits. I also saw the baby, who looked to me very much like any other baby."[6]

Mother and child were surrounded by too much love and affection for Susan Mary to feel hurt by her lover's cool attitude. She did not let herself criticize him, nor did she reproach him for his absence from the baptism ceremony a few months later. "Come if you can, my love, but I shall well understand if you can't."[7] Perhaps she chose not to heed Duff's indifference in the hope that he would change with time, that an older child would command more attention than a baby. She never failed to write about Billy in the letters she sent Duff, challenging his attention with a cheerfulness that sometimes felt slightly forced. She would pretend the baby had opinions and judgments of his own, and describe how he mastered tears and smiles, how he was taciturn but perceptive, impatient to grow and leave the restricted state of babyhood behind him. After all, didn't his godfather, Joe Alsop, call him a wunderkind? It was quite certain that he would have an exceptional future. She told Duff that Billy would become "an emperor of the Western Empire. Pax Pattenia. Civis Americanus sum. I love you."[8]

Because mere descriptions were not enough, Susan Mary sent photographs, handprints, and footprints. The resemblance between Duff and the baby that so pleased the young mother had not gone unnoticed. After telling Evelyn Waugh that Dolly Radziwill thought the baby was "a real little Noailles," and that Gaston Palewski thought it was the spitting image of Duff himself, Nancy Mitford continued, "I was rather bored by them, as I'm sure S-M is very virtuous, so I said 'Well but Duff is the image of all babies.'"[9] Susan Mary would have been deeply hurt by these rumors of which she remained unaware. She had told her secret only to Marina Sulzberger, the wife of the prominent journalist, and to her dear friend Marietta Tree, who was Billy's godmother.

Susan Mary, little Billy, and Billy's English nanny, Miss

Clark, went to Biarritz on August 11. An English sense of climate is useful to appreciate the weather of the Basque country in southwest France, with its rainy summers and green valleys. Still, the rain stops often enough, and on one of these occasions, Susan Mary, an experienced swimmer, pedaled down to the beach and flung herself into the water. Immediately, a large man in a yellow beret blew his whistle and ordered her out of the ocean, telling her that it was not safe.

Nothing, not even the rain or the swimming ban, could cloud Susan Mary's calm happiness. She, Billy, and the nurse were comfortably settled in a little villa surrounded by pine trees. Her friends Marie de Maud'huy and Miguel de Yturbe had welcomed her and left her to rest with the baby. Billy slept out on the wooden balcony when it was not too cold. Life was simple. The house was sparely furnished, there were few visitors, and she spent her time reading G. M. Trevelyan's *English Social History* and a book by Henry Adams. Susan Mary confessed to Duff, to whom she wrote every other day, that Bill and Mrs. Jay were far from her thoughts, as was the Politburo. It had been two months since the Soviets had cut overland connections to Berlin, and the sky over the German capital was filled with planes for the airlift. A group landed every ninety minutes. Coming on the heels of the coup in Prague, this event quickened the formation of alliances and the creation of the Federal Republic in West Germany the following spring.

Bill arrived at the beginning of September with a friend from London, effectively bringing an end to Susan Mary's blissful solitude. Wrapped up in a pea coat, she braved the rain to go out and buy gin for the men. To be a more available hostess she decided to wean her son. "I shall miss having someone so pleased to see me five times a day,"[10] she wrote. Although Bill often annoyed her, she was moved to see him take the baby to the beach on a sunny morning and was heartbroken when he told her sadly, after a visit to a doctor in Bordeaux, that he was practically an invalid and would never be able to teach Billy outdoor games. Although every breath was a trial, he almost never complained.

Back in Paris on September 21, the Pattens spent the weekend with the Coopers at Saint-Firmin. Duff recited Keats's ode "To Autumn" to Susan Mary in the forest of Chantilly, where the leaves were turning rusty red. It was the beginning of their favorite season and they were together again.

From One Continent to Another

Mrs. Jay was getting older, but she continued to cross the Atlantic every summer to visit her daughter and son-in-law, verifying for herself, like the formidable Mrs. Newsome in Henry James's *The Ambassadors*, whether Parisian life had succeeded in corrupting the American innocents. She noted with bitter pleasure the considerable consumption of bourbon and the merry-go-round of marital infidelity among her daughter's French and English friends, approving of nearly none of them. Even Marietta Tree, whom Mrs. Jay had known as a child, was criticized for having divorced. Susan Mary had to remind herself of everything she owed her mother—the financial support, the summer house in Senlis—to keep from openly expressing exasperation. The birth of Billy, to whom Mrs. Jay showed a great deal of affection, had improved things, but relations remained strained, which Susan

Mary tried to make up for by being overly attentive and smiling too much. She was sure, she told Duff, that her own birth was merely due to a last-minute afterthought of her mother's, and not to a real desire to have a second child. At heart, she felt she had been unwanted.

In spite of having tremendous energy for a woman of seventy, Mrs. Jay no longer felt like managing money matters on her own. At the beginning of 1949, she asked Susan Mary to help her sell the Georgetown house that she had bought at the beginning of the war for her newlywed daughter. Susan Mary was reluctant to leave Paris, and she spent the entire voyage on the *Queen Mary* imagining Billy sick with a severe case of laryngitis and Duff in the arms of the lovely Maxime de la Falaise, his latest dalliance. Still, she was thrilled to be going home; she had not been back in America for four years.

In the spring of 1949, President Truman, who, to widespread astonishment, had just been elected over the Republican candidate, Thomas E. Dewey, was concluding negotiations among the United States, Canada, and ten Western European countries to form the North Atlantic Treaty Organization. It was the first time that the United States had taken part in a peacetime military alliance beyond the American continent. Unlike most of her friends, Susan Mary had hoped that Truman would win the election. She was not dismissive of the politician who many wrote off as an impudent little man with a nasal voice. She knew better than many Washington insiders how much Europe, fearing another war, wanted protection; although she was wary of America's tendency to fill, as she put it, the fountains of Baghdad with Coca-Cola, she supported the new administration's diplomatic muscle flexing. America had now embraced its new status as a superpower.

Wandering through the quiet streets of Georgetown, Susan Mary rediscovered places she had known since childhood, the unpretentious houses, and the maids sweeping doorsteps and waving hello as though she had never left. However, the little town on the banks of the Potomac was different: it had become the capital of the world. Optimism was perceptible, she wrote to Marietta. "Everyone is busy planning ahead and, unlike France, there isn't time to look back."[II] She was also surprised that people wanted to hear about France and asked for her opinions.

When Susan Mary had come back to Washington in 1942 after her marriage, people had soon noticed that she knew how to liven up a room without making a fuss. Since then, her skills had obviously expanded. Washington society was aware that she had made a name for herself in Paris. They knew of her connection to the Coopers and of Ambassador Caffery's dependence on her services as a hostess. They had often seen photographs of her in *Harper's Bazaar* and *Life*. In truth, they found her a changed woman. Her beauty was more polished. She had the kind of face that the fashion of the day preferred: black and white with a red mouth, carefully drawn eyebrows, and disciplined hair. Besides, she had become more outgoing, positively glowing. Was it Parisian dresses, motherhood, or something else that gave her such an air of contentment?

Susan Mary was very much sought after. Her mother, always dismissive, said it was only because she was new. When asked about life in Europe, she told stories about high society. There was Donald Bloomingdale's marriage to Bethsabée de Rothschild, the Bal des Oiseaux in Boni de Castellane's pink palace, weekends at Ditchley, and tea with the queen at Lady Salisbury's. She knew which couturiers European women preferred (Dior, Balmain, Balenciaga, Jacques Fath) and what people were reading (Sartre and Camus, authors she herself had discovered with interest). She had seen Genet's *Les Bonnes* and the premiere of *Les Fourberies de Scapin,* featuring Christian Bérard's black and gray sets (he died almost immediately afterward, practically onstage).

For those who preferred politics, Susan Mary could talk about friends such as Lord Rothermere, the owner of the *Daily Mail;* Walter Lippman; Raymond Aron; Cy Sulzberger of the *New York Times;* and Frank Giles, who was a correspondent for the *Times* of London. Based on conversations with political leaders, she told the Washington elite that civil peace and political stability had nearly returned in France with Vincent Auriol and Henri Queuille, and that although General de Gaulle's supporters numbered nearly a million, Colonel Passy had assured her that his chief had no desire to become a military dictator. Things were starting to get better in France, she said. Bread was no longer rationed and the same would soon be true for gasoline. Still more astonishing, the French, who were the primary beneficiaries of American aid after the British, knew what they owed America. Maurice Petsche, the French finance minister, would soon recognize this publicly.

She spoke so well that Senator Henry Cabot Lodge wanted more and asked her to lunch at the Senate, an invitation she playfully mentioned in a letter to Duff. "I thought that would give you a laugh, and I know it will give Bill a sleepless night. I will be prudent and precise and only exaggerate when necessary."[12] In fact, she was quite proud of the stir she was causing. One evening at Ditchley the previous year, her friend Franklin D. Roosevelt Jr. had observed, "You and Marietta have certainly got around plenty since I was cutting in on you in Northeast Harbor."[13] It was true. Both had really come a long way. Marietta, however, had had the help of a wealthy husband, whereas Susan Mary had relied only on herself—her intelligence, curiosity, and energy. She was not displeased with the person she had become, and rightly so. If she had kept something of the candid excitement of a Jamesian heroine, she had also, unlike Isabel Archer or Daisy Miller, survived Old Europe. She had even, modestly but undeniably, been a success.

"Write to us all, Nanny and Duff and me, we love you in that order."[14] Bill's appeal worried his wife. Had Duff made an incautious remark? On her return to France at the end of March, she was relieved to find that nothing had changed. Duff and Bill had seen each other regularly during her absence, as they always had. In April she set off for England, where she made a round of visits to the dukes: Portland, Rutland, and Devonshire. The latter gave her a tour of his garden, sparing not a single daffodil, showing Henry VII's prayer book, and quivering with mock rage when two nuns ("Papists!" he shouted) wandered onto one of the park's tree-lined paths. Derbyshire, green and gray with grazing sheep and Friesian cows, reminded her of Jane Austen. Bill had just finished treatment in a London clinic. He joined her, and together they went on a tour of Ireland that took them to Dublin, County Limerick, and Derrynane, a town on the southwest coast; surrounded by camellias and magnolias, they spent three days there, during which Susan Mary did not write to Duff.

She stayed in Senlis all summer and did nothing much the following autumn because she had been expecting a child since spring and suffered from anemia and back problems. Anne was born at the American Hospital on January 20, 1950, smiling and lovely from the start. This time, the gossips had nothing to say.

Pretty Mrs. Jungfleisch

Pretty Mrs. Jungfleisch was deeply concerned about the present state of the world.[15]

—Nancy Mitford, *The Blessing*

One March evening in 1950, Bill and Susan Mary were having a martini before their guests' arrival. Susan Mary waited for Bill to start reading the paper. She lit a cigarette, and her heart began pounding.

"I had lunch with Duff and a friend of his today at the Tour d'Argent."

"What friend?"

"Oh, one of Duff's partners."

"What was he called? Annersley?"

"Probably. You know how Duff mumbles names."

"Was he amusing?"

"No, rather deadly, we talked about the movie business."[16]

The bustle in the front hall brought the conversation to an end. It had not gone too badly.

Although Susan Mary was an expert at the polite kind of lying through omission that is part of good manners, she was clumsier when it came to outright lies. Duff was indeed chairman of the

French branch of Alexander Korda's film production company; however, he would have never mixed business and lunch with a beautiful woman. Susan Mary and Duff had been at Lapérouse in a private room, where courtesans, testing their diamonds, had scratched their names on the mirrors like schoolchildren etching theirs on a desk with a pocketknife. Duff had a taste for the Belle Époque and loved the formality of grand restaurants and the atmosphere of the *maisons closes,* which, much to his regret, really had been closed. The combination of delights permitted by establishments like Larue, the Café de Paris, or Lapérouse suited him perfectly. "We were very happy," he noted in his diary that day, using one of his favorite euphemisms.[17] Unfortunately, on the way out, Susan Mary ran into a friend who was coming to dinner that very evening. She preferred to mention her lunch outing rather than chance an embarrassing remark in front of Bill. "I fear that I shall never be a skilled mistress, having lunch with you is still to me a desperate adventure."[18] Nevertheless, she took similar risks several times a month, meeting her lover in restaurants or in his apartment on the rue de Lille. A passionate letter followed every encounter, while Duff calmly noted that she was far more smitten than he was, and that he didn't deserve her. "I love her too, very deeply and tenderly. I am not 'in love' with her, although there is nothing I wouldn't do for her. I owe her so much."[19] Being in his sixties ("I hate my age") had not slowed his appetite for seduction or his desire for women. Durably attached to his mistresses, he cheated on all of them with a complete absence of scruple and tact. His only concern seemed to be a constant search for pleasure.

Susan Mary was wise enough not to probe her lover's true feelings too deeply or overanalyze their relationship. She knew she was loved, but she did not want to know where exactly she figured on Duff's list. When she heard rumors about supposed mistresses that she thought were untrue, she would tease him, purposefully getting it wrong. As to other, more dangerous women, she kept silent. She was convinced of being far less glamorous than his English girlfriends, whom she imagined splendid and sophisticated. Blaming herself for having "the bourgeois mentality of the Rangoon governor's wife,"[20] she felt fortunate to have ensnared a god. Did she realize passion was on her side only? If she did, she would have deemed it fair. Beside their secret bond, she was grateful to Duff for what he brought to her life: laughter, tenderness, and, above all, privileged access to his intimate knowledge of history and literature, two spheres he belonged to. In a moment of poor judgment she even claimed, "You are a better writer than old Balzac."[21] Duff guided her reading choices and they talked about them together. She may have exaggerated her ignorance, but she never feigned the joy she felt upon making it through difficult texts or discovering forgotten swaths of history.

All this reading and writing sparked off literary dreams. Her lover's identity and the epistolary nature of their affair began to evoke illustrious parallels. She saw herself as Lady Bessborough at the side of Ambassador Granville,[22] or as the Duchess of Dino—although, unlike Duff, Talleyrand had no mustache. These noble references peppered their correspondence with the magic of the past. Susan Mary began to pay closer attention to her style.

It was during this period that her life effectively passed from fact into fiction, but not quite in the manner she had hoped.

Although British novelist Nancy Mitford was a comic genius, she had little imagination. Her books read like her letters, and her letters resembled her conversation: brilliant, irreverent, confident, sometimes aggravating, always teasing, often to the point of cruelty. To her, serious matters were best left to bores and self-pity to chambermaids. Like Wilde, she transformed frivolity into art, and like Wodehouse, her books re-created a safe little universe that seemed untouched by the horrors of the contemporary world, a place where a lucky few cultivated wit as the highest form of civility. The milieu Mitford's books describe was very closely modeled on that of her family and friends.

Nancy Mitford had been in love with Colonel Gaston Palewski since she had met him in London in September 1942. She followed him to Paris, although she remained married to Peter Rodd. She lived in the same neighborhood as Gaston, but not in his house. "You know our cold respectability," he had explained, strictly forbidding her from moving into his apartment on the rue Bonaparte.[23] Nancy's love affair was not just with Gaston but with France in general and it would last until death. After her move to Paris, all her books were dedicated to her favorite country. *The Blessing*, published in 1951, celebrated France's superiority over England. According to Nancy, life in France was delightful, dowagers charming, women smartly dressed, religion tolerant, the sun always shining, politics intelligent, and men irresistible skirt chasers. Gaston figured in *The Blessing* as the idealized and charming Frenchman Charles-Edouard de Valhubert, a Gaullist, former member of the Resistance, collector of art and women, yet very fond of the Englishwoman he casually marries at the beginning of the novel. This satisfying fiction made up for the disappointments and sorrows of Mitford's real life, where Palewski remained as elusive as he was dissipated.

Susan Mary and Nancy knew each other fairly well. They met at the Coopers', at the Pattens', and at the lunches Nancy gave at her house on the rue Monsieur. Both shared a passion for the old, silent Paris captured by Atget, the still, private streets where foreigners rarely trod. Together, they had knocked on doors, opened gates, and, peering through windows, made out the sepia-toned light of inaccessible gardens. In the spring, they waited for the chestnut trees to bloom in ice-cream-colored shades of pink and white. After the dusty summer came the clear blue days of autumn, and later, the occasional bursts of winter light upon the gardens in the Tuileries. Paris had taken hold of their hearts.

Nancy gave Susan Mary a brief appearance in *The Blessing* under the name of Mildred Jungfleisch, a young, pretty, and earnest American woman who talks only "about conferences and vetoes and what Joe Alsop had told her when she saw him in Washington."[24] No doubt satisfied by this preliminary sketch, Nancy revived Mildred Jungfleisch in her next novel, *Don't Tell Alfred,* a book inspired by the guerrilla war waged by Diana Cooper against the unfortunate Lady Harvey, whose husband had replaced Duff as British ambassador. In the book, the new ambassador's wife is named Fanny, and her predecessor, Lady Leone. Described as the most beautiful woman in the world, Lady Leone secretly continues living in the embassy, assisted by her confidante, Mildred Jungfleisch, who sneaks in baskets of food and helps her entertain amused Parisians who desert the embassy's drawing rooms to line up at her door.

Mildred is described as belonging to a clan of Americans, "the Henry James type of expatriate, who live here because they can't stick it at home."[25] The new ambassador's wife tries to find a way to corrupt Mildred and rid herself of Lady Leone. With this task in mind, she questions one of her husband's aides about Mildred:

"What does she like best in the world?"

"English top policy makers."

"What, MPs and things?"

"Ministers, bankers, the Archbishop, Master of the Belvoir, editor of *The Times* and so on. She likes to think she is seeing history on the boil."

"Well, that's rather splendid. Surely these policy makers must be on our side? Why don't they lure her to England—luncheon at Downing Street or a place for the big debate on Thursday?"

"I see you don't understand the point of Mildred. They worship her at the House—they can hardly bear to have a debate at all until she's in her place there. She's the best audience they've ever had. As for luncheon at Downing Street, why, she stays there when she's in London."[26]

Although she had been cast as a blonde with a pageboy haircut, it was easy to recognize Susan Mary. Mitford's keen eye for character had captured her friend's devotion to Diana Cooper and taste for politics and intellectual aspirations, noting, "She puts aside certain hours every day for historical study."[27] Mitford also took aim at Susan Mary's popularity ("it was impossible to give a dinner party in Paris without her"[28]) and adaptability ("she could produce the right line of talk in its correct jargon for every occasion"[29]).

Although she seemed not to have recognized her cameo appearance in *The Blessing*, Susan Mary immediately identified herself in *Don't Tell Alfred* when the book was published in 1960. Accommodating and reasonably immune to vanity, she was nevertheless hurt to find her sentimentality and love of ideas ridiculed. Fortunately, Nancy did not know the lengths to which Susan Mary went in her desire to seem well informed. At the time, nobody realized, for example, that Susan Mary's letters to Marietta Tree were, occasionally, directly inspired by Janet Flanner's gin-soaked columns about Paris for the *New Yorker*. Mitford would have surely included this information with acerbic relish.

All the same, Susan Mary sent a few copies of *Don't Ask Alfred* to her friends. In truth, compared to other examples of wicked portraiture in which Nancy often indulged, Susan Mary's character had been gently crafted. It was almost flattering, more teasing than caricature.

The Blessing, nevertheless, had angered Susan Mary for its open anti-Americanism. Mitford was as virulent as a band of Stalinists in her hatred of the United States, a country she judged to be blundering, uneducated, and hideously modern. In her novel, she had concocted a talkative and self-important American named Hector Dexter whose job it was to persuade the recalcitrant French to swallow the bitter medicine of the Marshall Plan. The character was so grotesque and dislikable that Mitford turned him into a Communist mole to avoid being strung up by her

American friends. Still, there was an amusing truth in the portrait.

If Susan Mary had not liked the way Nancy had portrayed her countrymen, she was even angrier when her friend told her that the conversations she had heard around the Pattens' dinner table had helped her fine-tune horrible Dexter. Susan Mary had no illusions about her country and blamed America's lack of interest for all things foreign. She often mocked the grandiloquent style imposed upon American journalists, regardless of the context ("lots of words like history-making, soul-stirring, breathless, and of course, hero used freely"[30]). Neither did she hold back from criticizing American doings she found absurd, such as the government's distribution of cotton togas to several elected officials in the spring of 1950, supposedly as protection against radioactivity in the event of a nuclear war. She was shocked by Wisconsin senator Joseph McCarthy's anti-Communist witch hunt that had begun in the State Department, and by the news that General MacArthur considered using the atomic bomb against China at the end of 1950 in retaliation for its involvement in the Korean War. In spite of all this, she felt that no foreigner, let alone Nancy, who had never set foot in America, had the right to be so negative. Their friendship grew distant, but pretty Mildred, "this ghastly pedantic blue stocking bore of a Mildred Youngfleisch,"[31] as Susan Mary would say with a sigh, had been immortalized.

In Sickness and in Health

Regular routines have a bad reputation and are rarely celebrated by those who practice them. Susan Mary complained at times

about the monotony of her life, judging it to be useless, especially
when she compared herself with her friend Marietta Tree, who
had returned to New York and become an activist for the
Democratic Party. "I am sick of running a travel agency," she told
Marietta. "You do so many things of use and importance. I sit
here and, except for an absorbing life with my two little children,
the rest is meeting trains and making hotel reservations for the
mothers of girls I didn't even like at school and taking them to
the American Hospital when they have acute appendicitis, which
turns out to be overeating half the time."[32] She also regretted that
Bill had obliged her, in the name of the professional discretion
imposed on all diplomats' spouses, to turn down the offer to write
a weekly column for *Harper's Bazaar*. Invited to inaugurate a
community center near Lille in the presence of the French health
minister, she went off, trembling, in a pretty hat and came back
in high spirits, basking in the warm welcome her accent and
carefully rehearsed speech had received. "That's the life for a
woman. How sad to have had a taste of it just one sweet hour and
now back to doing up Anne's nappies."[33]

Susan Mary loved taking care of her children even though, if
truth be told, she rarely changed their diapers herself. As sincere
as her regrets about not having a career of her own might have
been, they remained periodic and rarely troubled her serenity. The
atmosphere at the embassy and the nature of Bill's work had
changed for the better since their arrival. In May 1949, the
Francophile David Bruce, who until then had been head of the
French branch of the Marshall Plan under the overall European
supervision of Averell Harriman, replaced Ambassador Caffery.
Chip Bohlen became his number two. David and his second wife,

Evangeline, and especially Chip and Avis Bohlen, were old friends of the Pattens. Much to Bill's delight (for he had grown weary of economic and financial questions), Chip took him on as part of his team. As Susan Mary began her sixth year in France, she had only one wish: that Bill's position—secured by her efforts, divine providence, and the State Department—continue on an even course. But turbulent changes were on the way.

The first incident was not too serious. The Aldrich cousins had decided to take back the house on the square du Bois de Boulogne so that they could rent it at a better price. This was fair enough, but it created a problem, because the postwar Parisian housing crisis was still very much a reality. Hearing the news, their circle of friends came together to help. There were some grandiose plans, including an apartment in the Hôtel Lambert, but this never came to fruition. Finally, in April 1950, the Pattens found a house on the rue Weber, just steps away from their former home. The children would be able to continue playing in the Bois de Boulogne. While she was waiting for her furniture to arrive from the United States, Susan Mary amused herself by cobbling together a sitting room à la Pompadour and a Three Musketeers–themed dining room with the help of shabby old cinema sets, which she rented in a rare and deliberate spate of bad taste that appalled the nanny, Duff, and Charlie de Beistegui.

Then Bill fell badly ill at the beginning of June. What began as pneumonia evolved into heart failure. Dr. Varay came to the house morning and evening. One of Bill's legs was paralyzed and a pacemaker was put in his bedroom. An English specialist was called in for a second opinion and recommended that Bill be transported to London for a bronchoscopy, a plan that Dr. Varay opposed. Trying to keep herself from panicking and painfully aware of her ignorance in such matters, Susan Mary decided that Bill would stay in Paris. His condition varied constantly. He often had trouble breathing and this made his pulse race even faster. Suffering led him to utter spiteful remarks, which Susan Mary bore without answering back, sad to see him grasp so hopefully at each minor and passing remission. At night she wrote to Duff, and sometimes, while Bill was sleeping in the bedroom next door, she called him on the telephone and wept uncontrollably. After ten days, the worst was over. It was decided that Bill and Susan Mary would leave for the United States on July 1 so that Bill could undergo treatment at the Lahey Clinic in Boston.

In the early 1950s, steroidal treatments were just beginning to be used in America. They worked quite well on Bill, and soon he was strong enough to play canasta and alternate between cortisone and Veuve Clicquot. Surrounded by family and friends, Susan Mary felt safer than in Paris, even though she had to placate Mrs. Jay and Mrs. Davies, who hated each other so much that each of them had brought a wheelchair for Bill's arrival, neither of them trusting the other to do so. Susan Mary also noticed that several friends who came to visit seemed moved by one of the rarer emotions of the human soul, that strange, secret pleasure taken from seeing somebody, particularly a loved one, suffer.

The doctors said Bill might live another four years. "I personally think I would rather not have my life prolonged, he is different from me," remarked Susan Mary, not without a certain harshness.[34] She was amused to see the doctors' perplexity when confronted with young Billy's perfect lungs. "All their ideas on asthma heredity are upset and they are writing learned papers for the medical journal on him."[35] One question gnawed away at her but remained unasked: would they be able to return to Paris?

After two weeks in Boston, the doctors allowed Susan Mary to take Bill to Bar Harbor, where the children were already waiting. The solidly constructed house had held up against the passage of time and the ocean winds. For once, Susan Mary found it a welcoming shelter and even approved of the old-fashioned carpets and muted colors of the William Morris wallpapers. Set up in a second-floor bedroom, Bill spent his days on the balcony, away from the children and the nanny's pitiless war against the rest of the household staff. Susan Mary left all decisions to her mother. She protested only once when 250 missionaries from one of the charitable organizations her mother sponsored held a meeting in the sitting room. This was all right, but when they began singing "Onward, Christian Soldiers" at the tops of their lungs, it launched Bill into heart palpitations.

Soon Bill was able to move around, and he began to take drawing classes with an eccentric local artist who crept about town in a velvet vest and floppy cravat, like a character out of *La Bohème*. When Susan Mary watched her husband in the harbor, drawing the rocking fishing boats in happy concentration, the pressure she had been feeling since his health had deteriorated began to subside.

Bill had to return to the Boston clinic twice for checkups and spent a few days in a local hospital to have an abscess looked after that had formed "from having had so many shots."[36] The doctors decided that he did not have lung cancer and that the Pattens could return to Paris. And returning to Paris meant being near Duff again.

So Bill recovered, resuming a more or less normal existence, and was even able to go to Italy twice the following year. In May 1951, he and Susan Mary went to Rome to visit Bill's sister, who had married an Italian. They met the black nobility, who lived in the Vatican's august shadows, the aristocrats in their palaces, and Princess Bassiano, who was trying to revive lyrical poetry with her review, *Botteghe Oscure*. For the length of their ten-day visit, the Pattens were all the rage. One of her admirers told Susan Mary, "Madam, everyone has been saying that with five kilos more you would have a tremendous success in Rome."[37] That spring, however, everybody's eyes were turned to Venice.

"I feel like Stendhal's young hussar in *Le Rouge et le Noir* trying to describe the battle of Waterloo,"[38] began Susan Mary's account of the party given in the Palazzo Labia by Charlie de Beistegui on September 3, 1951. Twenty years later, Paul Morand would echo her words, "An Italian ball, like in Stendhal!"[39] Cocteau noted, "Socialites don't understand the secret of theatre—what is striking and what isn't. According to the magazines, it would seem that Diana, Elizabeth, and Daisy wore their costumes well."[40] Morand was there, Cocteau was not. Neither was Nancy Mitford—she had not wanted to spend two hundred pounds on a costume. But Jacques Fath came as the Sun King in white and gold, along with Chilean billionaire Arturo Lopez, who was disguised as a Chinese ambassador, and Marie-Laure de Noailles, who was dressed as the Lion of the Piazza San Marco. Other guests were Leonor Fini, Orson Welles, Gene Tierney, Dalí, Dior, Cecil Beaton, Christian Millau, Deborah Devonshire, the Marquis de Cuevas and his ballet company, the Aga Khan and his wife, and Venetian firemen dressed as harlequins. It was a mélange of fine old names and new money, young beauties and aging beauties, celebrities from two continents. Seven hundred people came to the ball, which their unsmiling, white-wigged host had wanted to be as splendid as in the old times, when the Serenissima reigned unchallenged.

A number of *tableaux vivants* were indeed striking. There was Diana Cooper as Cleopatra, right out of the Tiepolo fresco in the palazzo's main hall, and Elisabeth Chavchavadzé, magnificent as Catherine the Great. Daisy Fellowes, wearing an enormous feather on her head, claimed to be the incarnation of the pre-Columbian Americas. Susan Mary had watched Diana get dressed. While Cecil Beaton and Oliver Messel transformed her into the Egyptian queen, Diana sewed a little bag for Duff's domino so he could keep his flask and not risk running short of alcohol. This turned out to be unnecessary, for the banquet was sumptuous like everything else. Susan Mary noted with admiration that even the shoes seemed historically authentic. She and her friend Odette Pol-Roger had decided on simple dresses and handsome velvet masks from Reboux. At three in the morning, Susan Mary went to bed, but Odette continued dancing to the accordion music among the crowds on the piazza, where the ball had overflowed into the Venetian night.

A few days later, there was another party in the Palazzo Volpi, where Susan Mary ended the evening on a sofa next to Duff, barely keeping a proper distance. But best of all was an outing to

Torcello. At the end of the year, she wrote to her lover with a list
of resolutions:

    1. To have you well and see you as much as possible
    2. To have Bill have less asthma and be happier
    3. To have Nanny less beastly to Edmond[41]
    4. To have Edmond less beastly to Nanny
    5. Not to be kicked out of this house
    6. To go to Venice again.[42]

When Shadows Fall

Life Without Duff

Retirement has advantages. It gave Duff more time to read and write, and his literary production became quite regular. In 1949, he published a short essay, *Sergeant Shakespeare*, followed by *Operation Heartbreak*, a novel inspired by a true story from the war. Then he set about writing his autobiography, a project that he saw as both testimony and revenge. Work went slowly, because the sources he needed were often hard to find and the prime minister's office was closely monitoring everything he wrote. It annoyed Duff, who knew time was limited. One August evening in 1951, after a dinner at Susan Mary's house in Senlis, he got a nosebleed that lasted for several days. This initial warning caused him to change his ways, but last-minute sobriety could not make up for a lifetime of excess; his liver and kidneys were in a sorry state. Duff suffered a second severe hemorrhage in May 1953 and was swiftly taken to a hospital, where he was saved by blood transfusions. He was not able to attend the June 2 coronation of the young Princess Elizabeth, although his recent elevation to the peerage and new title, Viscount Norwich of Aldwick, meant he had a reserved seat in Westminster Abbey. Many households purchased their first television sets for the coronation and screens were set up all over London. Like twenty million other English subjects, Duff had to be satisfied with watching from afar.

Susan Mary was somewhat luckier on that rainy morning. Isaiah Berlin gave her his place at one of the windows of the War Office, from which she was able to see the scarlet and gold procession of Queen Victoria's great-great-granddaughter to Westminster Abbey. *Vivat Regina*. The English monarchy knows how to put on a show, and although Elizabeth II was no longer empress of India, the ceremony kept enough of the old imperialist flavor to remain dazzling. The same day, London learned that a New Zealander and his Nepalese guide had conquered Mount Everest for the first time. It was a victory for the Empire that had been rebaptized the Commonwealth.

Duff's memoirs were published at the end of 1953 under the title *Old Men Forget* and were well received, apart from a few snide remarks exchanged between Nancy Mitford and Evelyn Waugh. The Coopers had been invited to Jamaica to celebrate the New Year, and they were getting ready for the voyage, which the doctors had approved. Sunshine would benefit Duff's health. They had lent Saint-Firmin to the Pattens, who were spending the holidays with Joe Alsop, the Sulzbergers and their children, David and Marinette, and other friends. A few days before Christmas, Duff and Susan Mary went shopping and bought a green velvet handbag for Diana. They had a drink and Duff gave Susan Mary a lesson in international relations. John Foster

Dulles, Eisenhower's secretary of state, had been threatening the French with an unfavorable shift in American policy if they did not overcome their divisions and their fear of German rearmament and ratify the European Defense Community. Supported by the French president of the council, René Pleven, and inspired by the ideas of Jean Monnet, this project for a common European army was intended to be an extension of the Schuman Declaration, which had created the European Coal and Steel Community and had managed to overcome opposition from Gaullists, Communists, and steel manufacturers. Duff was in favor of the EDC, as were Bill and Susan Mary, but he regretted Dulles's clumsy shakedown of the French government, even though the project had been lame for eighteen months, with nobody in France daring to present the plan for consideration before the National Assembly. The conversation then turned to lighter subjects. They talked about the Coopers' upcoming cruise, which Duff was looking forward to and Diana was dreading, although nobody understood why. She usually loved travel.

On New Year's Eve, a radio message arrived in Saint-Firmin asking if the Pattens could send Dr. Varay, the doctor who had cared for Bill, to Spain. Duff was suffering a serious relapse and the ship they had boarded the previous day was going to change route to drop them off at Vigo. Then John Julius, the Coopers' son, called. Duff had hemorrhaged to death while still at sea, and they had decided to repatriate his body to England by air. Fog ultimately forced the plane to land at Le Bourget, outside Paris, and Diana spent the night with the Pattens, soothed by tranquilizers and Bill's comforting words.

To suffer in secret is harder to bear than official mourning.

Susan Mary's sense of propriety and respect for Diana were far too strong to allow her to express more grief than the rest of Duff's friends. Still, she was touched by John Julius's gesture when he asked her to spend a few moments alone with Diana on the morning of the funeral. Afterward, Susan Mary blended into the crowd of mourners who had gathered at the Duke of Rutland's, where Duff was buried on January 6, 1954, and at the public service held the following day at Saint Margaret's in London. There were many French and British obituaries full of praise, except for the *Times,* which, to Susan Mary's indignation, criticized Duff's dilettantism. It did her good to have something to be angry about. Talking kept her from crying, and fretting from thinking too much.

In March, reprising her role as Mildred Jungfleisch, she accompanied Diana to Greece. They visited Corfu, Athens, and Olympia with its blue irises and anemones, went to Delphi (in the company of the writer Roger Peyrefitte), and the Cyclades. Diana sometimes managed to forget her sadness, and would recite the genealogy of the gods as they bounced up and down in tightly packed buses on tiny roads meant for donkeys. Transported by the smell of wild thyme, Susan Mary idly talked about buying a villa, and reserved a caïque and a crew of two men for the month of September. Diana was amused by her friend's unbridled excitement, and the sound of Susan Mary's schoolgirl's voice carefully reading the guide helped dry her tears. After three weeks of travel, Susan Mary returned to the bitter cold of France. Her life suddenly seemed empty.

Of course, there were the children to comfort her. Anne was chubby, happy, and easy to deal with. Billy was more intense.

Given to temper tantrums, he was nevertheless full of affection and goodwill. He had trouble adjusting to his strict French school, but he loved having stories and poetry read to him. A French governess named Mademoiselle Ogier had replaced the English nanny, and Billy and Anne became true French children, saying *ooh là là* and *dis donc,* solemnly shaking hands with adults, and viewing American food with dismay. Billy nearly fell off his chair in a Maine restaurant when he saw a plate of cranberry jelly covered with orange mayonnaise. "Look at that, Anne. It's called 'salad' in America. Can you believe it?"[1] he loudly exclaimed. Susan Mary had wanted her children to be familiar with French culture, but she had also hoped her son would learn English manners. At her request, Duff had enrolled him at Eton. What was to be done now that Duff was gone? The worst of it was that little Billy had shown a genuine and at times embarrassing liking for his mother's friend, answering the phone *"C'est toi, Duff? Ici Billy,"* kissing Duff's photos in albums ("Merry Kissmas, Duff"), and asking his mother, "Is Duff as good as he is pretty?"[2] Bill took no offense at any of this, simply remarking that Billy was "only interested in Duff and motor-cars."[3]

In spite of the tenderness she felt for Billy and Anne, Susan Mary had been more at ease as a mistress than as a mother, as she had often confessed to Duff. "Suppose I had to choose right now, never seeing Duff again or never seeing my children, there seemed to be only one choice, not even a hesitation. Poor little things, I do love them too."[4] The choice had been made for her. She was alone now, she who had written after a few weeks of summertime separation, "I have just about reached my maximum Dufflessness."[5]

The Fine Art of Memoranda

Susan Mary is said to have sat up in bed at the American embassy writing memoranda.[6]

—Letter from Nancy Mitford to Gaston Palewski,
December 6, 1956

Fortunately for Susan Mary, the world was still full of seemingly unsolvable problems. Her reason for existence had disappeared with the death of her lover, so she shifted gears and became more interested in international affairs than ever. In her own manner, she tried to do her part. Respectful of official hierarchies to the point that her insistent and unfaltering praise of all American ambassadors' wives in Paris seemed at times insincere, Susan Mary knew all the same that she was a fixed point in a shifting diplomatic universe. Intimate knowledge of French politics, customs, and sensitivities had given her a kind of status. As the corridors of power remained out of reach to all but career diplomats, she cast her nets in Parisian salons. Sidling up to the man she had singled out, she would engage him in conversation. Her voice would descend a pitch, her brows furrowed with interest, and she would tilt her head in a pose of absorption. Fingering her pearls, she would murmur, "How fascinating." Her favorite moments were those when she acted as a go-between, discreetly passing on messages. In addition to this diplomacy of whispered asides, she analyzed the political situation in her letters to Marietta Tree in the hopes that her friend, who was a Democratic Party supporter and very close to Adlai Stevenson, would put the knowledge to good use. Without exaggerated illusions about the importance of her role, Susan Mary continued to dedicate herself to these causes with the bubbling eagerness that Duff's teasing had never managed to dampen.

One of Susan Mary's goals was to improve relations between the French and the Americans, an increasingly difficult task as French prosperity and self-confidence returned in the early 1950s. Raymond Aron described the French rejection of all things American as "pathological" in a conversation with Susan Mary. It was an attitude that came in waves. In 1950, Coca-Cola had become public enemy number one. The French Communist Party claimed the Marshall Plan had been created to increase the consumption of the unhealthy soda, the distribution network of which was purportedly used by spies. *Le Monde* took the hysteria even further. According to Janet Flanner, "What the French criticize is less the drink itself than the civilization, the style of life of which it is a sign and in a certain sense a symbol. The very soul of their culture is in danger."[7] In November 1952, Eisenhower's election set off another round of anti-American tirades. Eisenhower was initially popular as the supreme commander of NATO's SHAPE,[8] but was criticized later for making comments during his presidential campaign on France's supposed moral decadence. When *Paris Match* published a list of the main things that the French disliked about Americans' living in France, it included too many people riding in powerful cars, lack of support in French Indochina in spite of France's effort to defend the "free world," and America's rigidly anticolonialist and hysterically anti-Communist attitude. Although, strangely enough, the Communist newspaper *L'Humanité* was the only French newspaper that did not cover the exploits of Senator McCarthy's anti-Communist witch hunt, it derided the United States daily. In the spring of 1953, shortly before the executions of Julius and Ethel Rosenberg for espionage, Paris was plastered with posters depicting President Eisenhower, his broad jaw lined with electric chairs instead of teeth.

To Susan Mary's eyes, part of this criticism was legitimate. The Pattens knew many diplomats who had suffered from the State Department's incessant anti-Communist investigations. Chip Bohlen, for instance, had gone through a humiliating interrogation when he was named ambassador to Moscow. Still, America could not be boiled down to a list of regrettable excesses, Susan Mary explained to the head of France's national police. She also defended the virtues of the Marshall Plan to the Duke de Luynes, who had attacked the American program as virulently as if he had been a French Communist Party member. But just when she thought she had convinced General Alphonse Juin of the soundness of Eisenhower and Dulles's policies, she discovered he had given a particularly virulent anti-American speech the following day. Her powers of seduction had limits.

In 1954, plans for the European Defense Community ultimately fell through, and the French Indochina War came to an end. Susan Mary had followed the unfolding of both events with intense interest. She kept Marietta up to date on the parliamentary crusade led by the center and the right-wing parties in favor of a European army until a breach of procedure brought ratification to an anticlimactic halt on August 30, 1954. She had realized how serious the Indochinese situation was when, at the end of December 1953, Joe Alsop asked her to tell Dulles about his conversation with Georges Bidault: Bidault had begged the United States to get involved in the war for fear that it would otherwise be lost. Susan Mary sent a telegram through the embassy, and Dien Bien Phu stuck in her mind. "I don't like the sound of it," she wrote to Marietta.[9] A few weeks later, the name became familiar to the entire world as the site of the final French defeat, which happened just before the Geneva conference that had been scheduled in hopes of resolving the conflict.

Two days before the conference, on April 24, 1954, the Pattens were invited to dine at the British Embassy. They had a drink with Foreign Secretary Anthony Eden, who returned to London to be told by Churchill that the British would not come to the aid of the French garrison under Viet Minh fire at Dien Bien Phu. "I sat by Gladwyn talking about the French theatre, imagine my frustration," wrote Susan Mary to Marietta, "but I don't know him well and dared not ask any questions."[10] At dawn on May 7, the final French defenses were overrun. "Strange that we foreigners should feel so shaken by the fall of a little French fortress in the jungle thousands of miles away."[11] Susan Mary did not know what to think about the American position on the issue, which had been divided and hesitant to the very end, but she admired the determination with which Pierre Mendès France, the new president of the council of ministers and French minister for foreign affairs, had found a solution to the conflict at the conference. She thought Mendès France an extraordinary man and rightly imagined that he would not last long as head of the French government.

Things were beginning to change in the old city of Paris. In March 1956, the Préfecture forbade animal-drawn vehicles in the city center during the day. The 500,000th Renault 4CV, an iconic French car, was proudly displayed at the Trocadéro, across from the Eiffel Tower. More and more French households purchased refrigerators, and the young Brigitte Bardot and Françoise Sagan were brazenly putting their elders out of style. But the essentials that had charmed or intrigued Susan Mary for more than ten years remained the same—the noisy animation of the place de la Contrescarpe, the existence of things like a state school for slate-tile roofers in Angers, the population's continual griping about politics and politicians, and the openly recognized right of everyone to have an opinion on everything.

"The dentist is quite apt to quote Baudelaire, the grocer is an expert on proportional representation, the politician wants to talk about the Proust exhibition at the Bibliothèque Nationale, and the priest compliments you on your dress and says, knowledgeably, 'Dior, n'est-ce pas?' (Of course this is a fashionable dining-out abbé, not a worker-priest or a country priest)."[12] What she loved, simply put, was the French art de vivre; it had survived for so long and was still holding on.

The merry-go-round of the Parisian social calendar continued. On February 14, 1956, Marie-Laure de Noailles gave a ball in her town house. The parquet was covered with playing cards, and 340 people were invited and told to come disguised as artists. Susan Mary had attended the countess's previous ball with Bill, but this time he was too tired, so she took one of Marietta's cousins, dressing him up as Edgar Allan Poe. Siezed by a sudden moral fit just before stepping into the party, the young man began spouting off about rebels in Algeria and the French homeless looked after by charismatic Abbé Pierre. Susan Mary whacked him over the head with the stuffed raven that was part of his costume and told him to keep his opinions to himself. "One comes to Europe to see the sights."[13] A repentant Poe mounted the grand staircase to the fanfare from *Aïda* with Susan Mary on his arm and the bird back on his shoulder.

Susan Mary had a talent for turning such events into cultural homework, interweaving frivolity and reporting. Dancing never kept her from investigating. She was keenly aware of the situation in Algeria. The French ties to that country seemed to her as obvious and respectable as the need for reforms. She had little patience for ideological simplifications and for the moralizing attitude of her countrymen, such as young John F. Kennedy, who explained one evening in Paris to an angry group of French people that the North African colonies ought to be given independence at once. She almost understood Odette Pol-Roger, who had felt like slapping the ignorant young congressman. In her own way, Nancy Mitford was no different. When an American asked her why the French preferred not to discuss the situation with his countrymen, she replied, "Well how would you like it if we began to interfere with your lynching arrangements?"[14] More serious minded than Nancy, Susan Mary deferred to Raymond Aron on the subject. In 1957 she warned Marietta that Aron told her he would soon be publishing a pamphlet showing that the Algerian War was ruining France financially and that the nation needed to prepare for Algeria's independence.

But nothing shocked Susan Mary quite as much as the Suez Crisis. In the fall of 1956, the French, British, and Israelis bombed and invaded Egypt to retaliate against General Nasser for nationalizing the canal. They finally had to back down when the

United States refused support and a Soviet ultimatum threatened missile attacks. Without much consideration for his British ally, Eisenhower put financial pressure on the British pound and considered stopping oil shipments. The crisis was felt less intensely in France, where the public's attention was diverted by the Red Army's crushing of the revolt in Budapest. In Britain, however, the government was split over the issue, and there was an uproar in the House of Commons, furious at having been excluded from the process. An ill and humiliated Anthony Eden went to Jamaica to recuperate, only to resign and leave the post of prime minister to Harold Macmillan on his return. During the entire month of November, Macmillan, who was then chancellor of the exchequer, repeatedly met with Winthrop Aldrich, the American ambassador to Britain, in an attempt to patch up relations with the United States.

As it happened, Susan Mary was also at the American Embassy in London, bed-ridden but alert to the situation. She had gone to London as she often did and dined with the Salisburys on the night of her arrival. Bobbety Salisbury, a member of Eden's cabinet, told her about the dramatic week; shaken by what she heard, she took a false step, fell down the stairs, and broke her elbow and collarbone. After a minor operation, she went to stay with her aunt, Harriet Aldrich, at the embassy.

Susan Mary's friends came to see her during her convalescence. Like them, she was appalled by the United States' lack of support. More clearly than the British, she drew conclusions from the affair. "The history books will write that this was Britain's last hurrah as an independent great power," she wrote to Marietta on November 26.[15] This was a perceptive view. A new age was beginning, during which the United Kingdom would see its boundaries limited to the shores of its small island. Mary Quant would give it color, blue jeans would trump tweeds, and "Rock Around the Clock" would drown out the strains of "Rule, Britannia."

May 1958

The French political crisis of May 1958 was pure adrenaline. Susan Mary and her friends Marina Sulzberger and Elise Bordeaux-Groult set up headquarters at the restaurant Chez Marius on the place du Palais-Bourbon. Excited like a trio of marquises during the Fronde, they ordered Charente melons and watched the skies, expecting General Massu's red beret paratroopers, who had already landed on Corsica on May 24, to drop out of them at any moment.

Paris too was waiting with bated breath. Policemen patrolled the streets. The French wondered what exactly was happening in Algiers; Americans, unsure whether there would be a civil war, spent their days between the radio and the telephone. On the evening of May 27, Susan Mary received a man sent by Joe Alsop, who had hastily come to Paris, and exchanged some of her francs for dollars, just in case. Cy Sulzberger recommended they keep the bathtubs full. At midnight, Susan Mary went downstairs and asked the cook to stock up on food.

On May 29, President René Coty addressed the French legislature, calling upon General de Gaulle, "the most illustrious of Frenchmen," to take the reins of the nation. That evening, the Pattens and Joe Alsop dined with friends who lived on the avenue

Gabriel. It was hot and the windows were open. Suddenly, a rumbling noise was heard outside and the dogs began to bark. The butler ordered the shutters closed. Susan Mary took off her jewelry and, leaving Bill behind, hurried into the street, pulling Joe along so insistently that he did not have time to put on his glasses. They headed toward the Elysée Palace, the official residence of French presidents. From a distance they could see the police barricades, and as they got closer, trucks full of soldiers armed with machine guns began to pull up. Joe could not hold Susan Mary back, and she ran, trying to get past the barriers. At moments like this, political drama seemed more erotic than love itself. A rumor spread through the crowd: General de Gaulle's supporters were parading nearby on the Champs-Élysées. Joe and Susan Mary found themselves caught up in the atmosphere of a Bastille Day celebration. A hearty blond woman took Joe in her arms, singing songs from the Liberation at the top of her lungs. Car horns blared and the crowd shouted "De Gaulle *au pouvoir.*" On June 1, the Chamber of Deputies invested General de Gaulle with executive power. The Fifth Republic would soon be formed.

Although Bill was as interested as Joe and Susan Mary were in the events of May 1958 and expected a positive outcome from the shift in power, his health kept him from following them into the streets to watch the coup d'état in action. The quality of his work and the fondness his supervisors felt for him (combined, perhaps, with Susan Mary's meddling) had kept him at the embassy until the end of 1954, after which he took a job at the World Bank. At the beginning of 1958, he had to retire. Emphysema, which alternated between violent attacks and periods of remission during which he convinced himself he might recover, dictated his entire existence. With the children he was always cheerful, a wonderful father full of jokes and amusing stories. He knew how to quiet a crying baby by swinging his gold pocket watch on its chain, how to teach a little girl to waltz and a little boy to play baseball. As often as he could, he visited Billy at his new boarding school in Beachborough, England (where he and Susan Mary had sent the boy in January 1958), even attending a cricket tournament on the school's famous pitch. When Anne came home from school, he used to welcome her by whistling the theme song from *The Bridge on the River Kwai* and supervise her homework. To help her learn multiplication tables he had crates of oranges delivered. "Nine times nine?" he would ask her, and Anne would gather up piles of fruit that had rolled all over the floor.

But Bill's charming dimples, humor, and courage could not hide his wheezing and the excess weight that began to pull at his suit jackets. Too often, his mouth twisted up in agony, his face changed color, and he would hurry, cane in hand, to his bedroom, where the indispensable oxygen tanks were stored.

In the apartment at 54, avenue d'Iéna, where the Pattens had lived since the spring of 1956, Anne's bedroom faced the courtyard and Billy's room looked out over the chestnut trees on the place des États-Unis across the avenue. His room was separated from his father's by a bathroom. A well-brought-up child never enters his parents' bedroom without a sense of dangerous transgression, even when invited to do so. For Billy, his father's room, with its perpetually drawn curtains, was a scary, dreadful place. The familiar clutter on the dresser and the pervasive smell of Old Spice was not enough to stave off the threatening shadows looming over the bed.

Susan Mary also tended to pause before entering Bill's bedroom. It seemed to her that she would rather find him dead than clutching in torture at the tubes of his rubber breathing mask. One July evening in 1958, she thought the end had come. Bill fell unconscious and was taken to Necker Hospital, where Susan Mary, Elise Bordeaux-Groult, and two nurses practiced artificial respiration on him for the entire night. When a second team came to take over their shift, Susan Mary and Elise, soaked with sweat, went to smoke a cigarette in the moonlit courtyard.

"Elise, we've lost the fight. Do you think I could ask these French doctors to give Bill a strong dose of morphine?"

"The hell you can. Just you wait."[16]

Later, as the Algerian families of wounded nationalist fighters could be heard wailing and singing in the halls, Elise, swearing like a sergeant major, dripping and determined, slowly brought Bill back to life.

It was only a deferral. Modeling herself on her stoic husband, Susan Mary accompanied him into a slower rhythm of life. Close friends came to visit: Diane de Castellane, who had married Philippe de Noailles; Dottie Kidder, whose husband worked at the embassy; Fred Warner, a young English diplomat; and of course Joe Alsop, who crossed the ocean to see his old friend Bill. Little Anne made a wonderful nurse, and in June 1959, she accompanied her father to the United States while Susan Mary escaped to England to visit her son. Bill's boarding of the ocean liner SS *Flandre* did not go without incident, and the other passengers had to make way for the "gallant buffoon," as he self-deprecatingly called himself. "Everyone I passed will, I feel sure, benefit from the sad brave smile I bestowed upon them and resolve to lead better, cleaner and more honourable lives."[17] He wrote playfully to his wife, "I have found nobody of either intellectual or sexual interest to arouse me from the state of lethargy I always fall into when we are separated."[18] Still in love, he reminded her that he was waiting for her letters and especially for her arrival. At the beginning of August, she joined him in Maine.

The English Lover

"My dear Susan Mary," began old Sumner Welles (who had served in the State Department under Roosevelt and helped Bill get his first job with the government), "I didn't put you beside me tonight to talk about my grandchildren, who interest neither of us. There are several things I want to find out from you, let's begin with this, what exactly do you think of Gladwyn Jebb?"

She remained silent.

"Come, come, you must know about Gladwyn Jebb, I'm told that he is the Foreign Office today. What would he feel about the Khrushchev conversation?"

"I haven't the faintest idea."

"This is very unlike you, my dear child, you always have ideas about everything."[19]

Sumner Welles was right. Susan Mary's silence was not due to her ignorance, but rather to the extreme caution that her host's keen perception required. It was out of the question that the good people of Maine should start whispering behind her back the way Boston society had done a few years before. And whisper they would have had they discovered, with horrified delight, that Bill

Patten's virtuous wife, Susan Jay's devoted daughter, Billy and Anne's loving mother, was yet again leading a dissipated and sinful existence, and, far from being tormented, thoroughly enjoying it.

The object of her affection was a certain Gladwyn Jebb. Born in 1900, he was appointed Britain's ambassador to France in 1954. Those who disliked him found him tactless, pompous, and cold. Nancy Mitford adored Jebb and praised his kindness to the heavens. Nobody questioned his rectitude and great intelligence, nor did they deny him courage, lined though it was with vanity. Jebb had made a reputation for himself as British ambassador to the United Nations during the Korean War when he faced down his Soviet opponent in a televised debate that turned him into an overnight celebrity. At the time, the always envious Evelyn Waugh remarked that Jebb thought of himself as Sir Galahad and lived like the Great Gatsby. Susan Mary didn't think much of him in those days either. "I remember Gladwyn as a cold poached egg type in Paris, and doubt if I will change my opinion," she wrote to Duff on September 20, 1950.

What brought about such a radical change of heart? Susan Mary must have found a certain professional and intellectual similarity between Gladwyn and Duff, even though Gladwyn was ten years younger and the two men had not been friends. Like Duff, Gladwyn loved books; Balzac and Chateaubriand were among his favorite authors. Like Duff, he thought that Britain would not be betraying its values if it turned toward Europe. Physically speaking, the two men were unalike, but they had similar careers, the same friends, the same beliefs, and the same clubs. Duff, it seemed, had branded Susan Mary's taste in men. When it came to love, she was an Anglophile and walked on Pall Mall.

Like Duff, Gladwyn was sentimentally stingy. He and Susan Mary had to be careful because Gladwyn's wife, Cynthia, did not practice the same open arrangements that Duff and Diana Cooper had. To even shake the foundation of the Jebb marriage would be inadmissible. Susan Mary understood these rules and adhered to them in principle. With Duff, she had learned to make do on meager rations, to be content with crying in her pillow after merrily parting ways with her lover on a street corner.

Even though Susan Mary's feelings were painfully hemmed in, they provided a welcome diversion from the sad, shrunken existence caused by Bill's illness. Before getting involved with Gladwyn, she had overcome, in part, the emotional widowhood caused by Duff's death by leading an amusing social life with intelligent people. That time had come to an end. Susan Mary needed more.

She took up letter writing again. Although her husband's imminent death did not drive her to despair, her days remained full of anxiety and torment. She had been raised to show nothing of this, and maintained a calm exterior out of pride and respect for Bill, so successfully that some described her as cold. Good manners, in her book, demanded permanent cheerfulness; however, she had grown weary of lies and polite smiles and was ready for something sweeter.

Beyond the desire to escape from daily life and the temptation to relive the joys she had experienced with Duff, there was real chemistry between Susan Mary and Gladwyn that, happily, cannot be explained. In July 1958, she felt, for no particular reason, filled with a sunny feeling and an indefinable tension every time a chance encounter caused her to cross paths with Gladwyn. A year later she would write, "I miss someone in Europe day and night."[20] She also quoted Benjamin Constant in French: "To love is to suffer, but it is also to live, and I hadn't lived for such a long time."[21]

A Release and a Sorrow

The summer of 1959 was a difficult time for poor Susan Mary in spite of the comfort she found in her lover's letters. It was tiresome to navigate the demands of her quarreling husband and mother and to take part in the tightly organized social life of Northeast Harbor, which felt at times like a summer camp for rich adults.

"We have sailing groups and rowing groups and mountain climbing groups and tennis groups, divided into different age groups. After two days here I awoke to the sound of pouring rain, the music of archangels couldn't have sounded sweeter to me, but the pursuit of pleasure is inexorable, it appeared that on rainy days group activities continue indoors, one learns to tie knots and so on."[22]

Above all, it was painful to watch Bill suffer. He could not go long without breathing from an oxygen tank, but he had given up very little of his usual occupations. As often as possible, he invited his friends to the house, went on picnics, and loitered along the ocean's edge to admire his wife and children swimming with baby seals. He even made a trip to Groton to show Billy the school he had so loved as a boy. (Billy was scheduled to begin studying there in the fall of 1961.) The variations of Bill's condition

Thirty-year-old Susan Mary posing for *Vogue* at her house in Paris, October 1948.

Susan Jay and her two daughters. Emily is standing and Susan Mary is in her mother's arms.

Susan Mary and her sister, Emily, in Buenos Aires. This picture was taken in 1926 during the last year of Emily's short life.

Susan Mary as a teenager.

Susan Mary as a young woman.

Susan Mary and her husband, Bill Patten, leaving
church after the marriage ceremony in Westbury,
Long Island, on October 28, 1939.
© *Bettmann/Corbis*

Lady Diana Cooper, Duff
Cooper, and Louise de Vilmorin at the Bal du Panache
in June 1947. Christian Bérard
had organized the ball and
put Susan Mary on the
committee.
© *Rue des Archives/AGIP*

Winston Churchill and Odette Pol-Roger at the Coopers' château in Chantilly, 1947.

Duff Cooper and Susan Mary at the Volpi ball in Venice, September 1951.

Duff Cooper, the British ambassador to Paris, and his wife, Lady Diana Cooper.
© *Hulton-Deutsch Collection/Corbis*

The Pattens' Christmas card from 1950. Anne is nearly a year old and Billy is two and a half.

Billy Patten at Chantilly in 1952.

The Duchess of Windsor and Pamela Churchill (who would later become Pamela Harriman) in Paris. Susan Mary was closer to the duchess than she was to Pamela Churchill.
© *Rue des Archives/AGIP*

The inimitable Joe Alsop.

Jackie Kennedy undertook a renovation of the White House on her arrival. She invited Susan Mary to be part of the project. Henry du Pont, standing behind Susan Mary, advised Jackie. Beautiful Babe Paley, wife of CBS founder Bill Paley, can be seen on the far right hand side of the picture. *William J. Smith, © AP Photo/Sipa Press*

President John Kennedy and Chip Bohlen, the American ambassador to Paris, in Palm Beach on April 16, 1963. Bohlen was a great friend of Susan Mary's. *© Bettmann/Corbis*

Marietta Tree, Susan Mary's dearest childhood friend. © *Bert Morgan Collection, © Getty Images*

Susan Mary at Marietta Tree's house in Barbados.

Susan Mary was very close to the elegant Evangeline Bruce, the wife of the American ambassador to Paris. © *Cecil Beaton, © Condé Nast Archive/Corbis*

Robert and Ethel Kennedy on their way to a dinner given by Susan Mary and Joe Alsop on the evening of June 18, 1967. © *Guy Delort, © Condé Nast Archive/Corbis*

General Westmoreland, Secretary of Defense Robert McNamara, and President Lyndon Johnson at a White House meeting, November 1967. © *Rue des Archives/AGIP*

Susan Mary knew President Nixon and got along well with his secretary of state, Henry Kissinger. © *Rue des Archives/RDA*

Susan Mary photographed for *Town & Country* in May 1992. © *Harry Benson*

annoyed Mrs. Jay, who grumbled, "One moment Bill is dying and the next he is ordering up champagne."[23] Susan Mary preferred to toast his courage and made sure her ministrations were never too visible, trying to avoid treating her husband like an invalid in front of their friends. Still, discouragement sometimes got the better of her admiration. When a famous Boston physician told her that her husband was slowly suffocating to death, she wrote, "I bitterly asked the doctor if it was worth prolonging this discomfort, stupid of me, of course one must, but it's hard to begin again."[24] Usually quick to feel guilt, Susan Mary did not blame herself for this particular disloyalty. Still, she never fell prey to the temptation to give up the fight, and ordered a new and improved respirator, "ruinous as usual and hard to get but surely worth it?"[25]

When they returned to Paris, Bill seemed to be doing better. They celebrated their twentieth wedding anniversary with a dinner for twenty-four during which he made a toast to Susan Mary that brought tears to her eyes. Not long thereafter, Dr. Varay, who had become a friend, confirmed the American doctors' diagnosis. He gave Bill three months to live. He was wrong, but by very little.

Long expected, played and replayed in gruesome rehearsals, the end came quietly. Spring had just begun, and on March 25, 1960, Bill was having a relatively comfortable day. Susan Mary took a walk and happened to see Khrushchev, who was visiting Paris. She went upstairs to tell her husband. Anne came home from school with good grades to show her parents. All three watched their new television together. That night, Bill fell into a coma. Susan Mary called a doctor who lived in the building, but it was too late. Bill's heart had given out and he died early on the morning of March 26, 1960.

In the days and weeks that followed, the children were a great comfort to Susan Mary. Anne and Billy kept themselves from crying, putting aside their own grief to take care of their mother. During the service at the American Cathedral in Paris, everybody noticed how tenderly they looked after her. For the first time in her life, Anne wrote a letter in English: "Dear Mummy, try to bee *raisonnable*. Everyone Love's *vous* and me the most of all."[26] When they went to bed, the children would set their alarm clock for eleven in the evening to wake up, go into their mother's room, and make her close her desk. One of them put out the lights, and the other opened the window. Susan Mary could not sleep (Gladwyn had forbade her from taking sleeping pills), but she did not dare get out of bed and contradict the orders of her guardian angels.

Her mother, on the other hand, was driving her crazy. Mrs. Jay never stopped making remarks in a stage whisper, taking the houseguests as witnesses, "Did you ever see anything so pitiful— so white—so fragile—so young?" Angrily, Susan Mary repeated her mother's words to Gladwyn, noting, "None of which is true. Young, *hélas* I'm not—pitiful—I won't be. Sad I am, not for Bill's dying but for his living so unhappily these last years. I tried and failed to make him share the fear and loneliness I saw so often in his eyes. A cleverer, more tactful woman could have helped him."[27] This secret torment, largely unjustified, never left her mind at peace.

Susan Mary was surrounded by well-wishers. Letters and flowers arrived every day from friends and relations in Paris,

England, and the United States. To her great joy, Frank Giles and
Bobetty Salisbury sang Bill's praises in obituaries for the *Times* of
London. At Easter, the Sulzbergers took her with them to the
south of France for ten days, though the holiday did little for her
extreme state of apathy and fatigue. Friends came up with ideas,
usually advising her to live where they happened to be. Isaiah and
Aline Berlin imagined she would be happy in Oxford, Gaston
Palewski suggested Rome, Fred Warner recommended London
("you would grow plump and placid"[28]), while the Lippmans
leaned toward Washington and the Bostonians lobbied for
Boston. Susan Mary only felt like playing with Anne and Anne's
Labrador, or seeing Gladwyn, which was difficult. The ambassador
took the time, at Susan Mary's request, to write the children
affectionate letters. In May, Joe Alsop came to see her. The
following month she went to the United States for Bill's burial in
a cemetery near Boston at the top of a small hill planted with pine
and birch trees.

When she returned to France, Susan Mary rented a villa near
Hossegor, north of Biarritz, spending her time with the Bordeaux-
Groult family, Pierre and Elise, Timothy and Victoria, and Bobby
and Daphné. The weather was bad, and the children were often
sick and restless, but Susan Mary's strength began to return. She
went to see her friend Marie-Alice de Beaumarchais, and started
to take an interest in the upcoming presidential election in the
United States. When she returned to Paris in autumn, she
enrolled as an auditor at the École des Sciences Politiques. Very
Mildred Jungfleisch of her, was Mitford's comment, saying that
she would have to put it in the next edition of her book.[29]

Susan Mary's studies in political science were only an interlude

before she had to face the nagging questions about her future. The
writer Louis Auchincloss had congratulated her on the
magnificent creation that had been her life with Bill, in spite of
his illness. Isaiah Berlin also admired the family edifice she had
managed to build. What should she dedicate her energy toward
now? Adlai Stevenson believed in her organizational talents,
although she felt she had none. She had little confidence in her
own courage and did not know what to do with herself and the
children. America seemed like the most obvious destination, but
was it the best? Did she want to remarry? Gladwyn had returned
to England, and in his letters he wrote that he imagined she
would settle down with an American senator. She found a letter
from Duff, written for her to read in 1960, at a time when he
expected both he and Bill would be dead. He said she should
marry a British ambassador to China or a secretary of state in a
new Russian-Atlantic alliance. It was all quite absurd. There were
no senators or secretaries of state lining up outside her door, just
three marriage proposals.

"Two are girlhood admirers who I should think would run a
mile if I accepted and they had to face the consequences, which
includes divorcing nice if dull wives, the other is unexpected."[30]

VII

At the Court of King Jack[1]

Joe Alsop's Victory

In theory, the Kennedys had the game in the bag. The family ship was poised to set sail, riding on the winds of paternal fortune, success in the primary elections, and Bobby Kennedy's effective war machine. But voters cannot always be controlled, and many of the party delegates who had gathered in the carnival-like atmosphere of the 1960 Democratic Convention at the Los Angeles Sports Arena still clung to their enduring affection for Adlai Stevenson, their losing candidate in the 1952 and 1956 elections. Warmed up in a standing ovation for Eleanor Roosevelt, who had chosen not to support John Kennedy, the delegates fell into a wave of hysteria when Stevenson's name was proposed for nomination. From the grandstands to the arena floor, the entire stadium swayed, repeating the candidate's name like a mantra, while the Stevenson majorettes threw caution to the wind and improvised a writhing war dance. Journalists who had already prepared reports on Kennedy's victory became concerned that their work was not over for the evening. But Bobby's army tightened ranks and Senator John Fitzgerald Kennedy was chosen by a broad majority. Tanned and handsome like an actor, he was a man of patrician tastes, if not of patrician birth. A veneer of wealth and his time at Harvard and in Great Britain had covered the traces of the Irish immigrant past—only Catholicism remained. He was a veteran of the Pacific war, obsessed with history, thoughtful when at rest, energetic in action, enthusiastic about his causes, tight-lipped about his secrets (womanizing and health problems). Kennedy had begun his campaign without support from liberals, farmers, unions, or black leaders, but his father and family stood behind him. At forty-three, he was much younger than the other Democratic candidates, and only his Republican opponent, the shadowy forty-seven-year-old Richard Nixon, was a little older than him.

Joe Alsop was pleased with Kennedy's nomination. His man had won the first stretch of the race to the White House. The next day, he and his friend Phil Graham, the director of the *Washington Post,* went to Kennedy's convention headquarters at the Biltmore Hotel to push for the nomination of Lyndon Johnson as the vice presidential candidate. Seated at his desk with his hands behind his head, a relaxed John Kennedy listened to the two journalists explain how Johnson, the Senate majority leader and a formidable politician, could bring in crucial Southern votes. During the discussion, Joe had the impression that Kennedy's mind was made up and that Johnson had already been chosen to share the ticket.

That summer, the Kennedy clan gathered at Hyannis Port as usual, with the difference that reporters were running around the property's beach, lawns, and patios. This did not bother Kennedy, who managed to keep ahead of them, going sailing when he felt like it, but it annoyed his wife, who was having trouble adjusting to the physical demands and constant exposure of her new public life. Joe was very fond of Jackie, and when he was invited to spend a weekend with the Kennedys at the end of July, he reasoned with her about her obligations and assured her that she was capable of meeting them. He had less success when it came to taking part in the athletic family's favorite pastimes. Holding Bobby's five-year-old son, David, by the feet, he swung him around until the boy hit his head on a ceiling beam.

David turned white and bit his lip, but he soon asked, "Can we do it again?"

"Of course," said Joe, who had gone even whiter than the child.

When Joe congratulated Ethel on her son's courage she simply remarked, "Oh, we don't allow crying. Do hold in your stomach, Joe."[2]

Observing the entire Kennedy family together was an awe-inspiring experience, "like Sparta," wrote Joe to Susan Mary.[3]

That summer, Joe Alsop's letters came one after the other, each more patient, gentle, and persuasive than the last. His words aimed for Susan Mary's heart, but they also found their way into her mind and touched her spirit. They told two stories. One was political. Although Joe had always declared himself a Republican and had voted for Eisenhower in 1952, he had come to think that the president was weak on national defense. So he had shifted his support to the Democrats, and particularly to Senator Kennedy, whose ascent he had watched with an interest that owed as much to Kennedy's charisma as to the firmness of his position on the development of America's nuclear arsenal. In turn, Kennedy was aware of Joe's potential impact as one of the most-read editorial writers in the country, under contract with the *New York Herald Tribune*, author of articles that appeared in nearly two hundred newspapers with a total readership of twenty-five million. What was more, Joe was cultured, funny, and seemed to know everybody through his Harvard, family, and professional connections. He gave great parties and was liberal with champagne, although Kennedy thought he did not invite enough pretty women. From early 1960 onward, the two men established a mutually beneficial relationship through meetings and conversations that Joe tried to play down to avoid attacks on his professionalism. He had no reason to hide this friendship from Susan Mary. Rather, far more openly and amusingly than in his columns, he wrote her a detailed account of JFK's unstoppable ascent, a subject that riveted the whole of America.

The second story in Joe's letters was rather more intimate and written in a very different, far less brazen tone. As humble as a pastor requesting a small donation to repair the church roof, who wrings his hands in anguish and is reluctant to cross the threshold of his wealthy parishioner's house for fear of being a bother, he wrote to Susan Mary in June 1960 to ask her to marry him. He explained that he had not dared to do so during his visit to Paris the previous month for fear that she would laugh in his face. For her sake, he would change careers and live wherever she wanted, even in Europe. He did not expect her to be in love with him. She would be free to leave him if she fell in love with somebody else. Better still, if she currently had a lover, which was likely—how else could she have made it through the torment of the past years—she was welcome to continue seeing him. Joe would put up with it. Finally, he told her he was homosexual.

Susan Mary's answer was prompt and firm: marriage was out of the question. But it took more than a polite refusal to discourage stubborn Joe. With the eloquence and obstinacy he had used to support America's entry into World War II, General Chennault's policies in China, the State Department's loyalty brought into question by McCarthy, and the existence of a missile gap, Joe set to work trying to change Susan Mary's mind. Although she said she would not marry him, she kept asking for political news, and he used this as an excuse to continue writing, pleading his case while mixing in politics and concocting a future in which Susan Mary, Joe, and Kennedy would rule Washington and, by extension, the world.

Joe's homosexuality was not discussed in Washington circles and most of his friends seemed to be unaware of it, apart from his brother Stewart. Although some may have had a suspicion, they kept it to themselves out of propriety, indifference, or embarrassment. To them, Joe was just a bachelor who had no girlfriend but liked beautiful and intelligent women. He adored risqué stories, and on hearing them, his eyes would sparkle behind his round glasses. Joe was also an excellent conversationalist if he managed to stay calm and not drink too much. He was a popular guest in Washington's best houses, and nobody called him, as Gore Vidal later did in one of his novels, the Baron de Charlus of Georgetown.

Yet the FBI and CIA knew that Joe had interests beyond collecting Bronze Age and Asian art. There had been two incidents of note. The most troubling one happened in Moscow in February 1957 when Joe fell into a trap laid by the KGB. After showing him photos of himself with a young man in a hotel room, the Russian agents proposed he collaborate with them, an offer Joe refused before being quickly shuttled out of the country by the American Embassy. Back in the States, Joe went straight to the FBI and told them what had happened. The affair ended there, but the KGB kept the photos, and J. Edgar Hoover kindly leaked Joe's FBI file to Eisenhower's staff. Some of them were tempted to use the information when Joe's articles became too negative, but this never happened. Still, the risk was always there.[4]

Joe's revelation came as a complete surprise to Susan Mary. She was both intrigued and touched by his openness. She asked Elise Bordeaux-Groult if she thought a marriage under such terms was possible. Without really understanding the significance of what Joe had told her, she interpreted his confession as a hint at a possible change in his nature. From the little he said about himself, she re-created him completely in her own imagination. Before his confession, she had known only his noisy triumphs, his clamoring affection, and the admiration he laid out before her like a luxurious sable coat. A new person seemed to appear beneath Joe's tough exterior, someone timid, lonely, vulnerable, in need of tenderness. At the age of fifty, it seemed he finally wanted to be like everybody else. Perhaps, she felt, it was her duty to rescue him, to take the hand he was holding out. Little by little, she overcame her misgivings and hesitation, and began to believe in the version of Joe suggested by his letters. At the end of the year, he came to see her in Paris, and it seemed her instinct was correct. In December she wrote to Marietta, explaining: "As the correspondence continued I began to know a new Joe that I didn't know existed and I began to think, oh, well, it would be a good idea for the children etc. and being a hopeless romantic couldn't make up my mind."[5] In the same letter, she announced that she had fallen in love with Joe and was getting married to him.

It is tempting to reduce Susan Mary's final consent after seven months of letter writing to a reasonable transaction between two people from the same social circle with the same tastes, memories, and ambitions. Many did. Indeed, both Joe and Susan Mary were far too realistic not to realize how beneficial the marriage would be. Joe would be provided with a family, one that he had always known. It was a social advantage and a personal comfort that improved his standing and respectability. Susan Mary would have a new home, enter a political clan, and become one of Washington's most sought-after hostesses—such was Joe's prestige and position in the community. She also knew that Joe loved her children and would make an excellent stepfather to Billy and Anne. As to the rest—oh well. She could do without it. She had already done without it for quite some time. Or maybe Joe would change.

Still, cold-blooded calculation alone does not account for Susan Mary's gamble in choosing to marry Joe. Neither of them could have imagined such an arrangement if they had not already been linked by an old and affectionate friendship. In a way, marriage seemed the next logical step. Bill Patten's memory also had an influence: Joe felt responsible toward the widow and children of his dead friend, and Susan Mary felt she could trust a man who had always been loyal to her husband. Finally, Joe's and Susan Mary's fantasies seem to have weighed on their decision. Joe, who knew women only in formal, social terms, had fallen in love with a vision more than with an actual person. He expected Susan Mary to conform to an impossible ideal of grace and intelligence. On her side, Susan Mary had given in to the charms of Joe's tender pleading, a tone she wrongly thought he would always use, and which was soon replaced by verbal sparring. Civilized camaraderie might have been an achievable goal for their partnership, but Susan Mary and Joe, although highly sophisticated, were both in their own ways romantic at heart.

Dumbarton Avenue

2720 Dumbarton Avenue was a plain yellow concrete cube, barely hidden by a curtain of ivy and clematis, a blemish on Georgetown's streets, which were lined with charming redbrick houses fallen out of a Victorian picture album. Deeming amateur architecture a gentlemanly pursuit, Joe had drafted the plans for the house when he bought the plot of land in 1949, and had immensely enjoyed the shock it gave his neighbors (they soon took measures to change local laws and make sure that a similar outrage would not repeat itself). Susan Mary could not help sighing at the sight of the building—"ugly as sin,"[6] in her opinion—but the spacious interior was more to her liking. The house's two wings surrounded a garden created by Bunny Mellon that contained eight different sorts of boxwood ennobling the little patch of green with their geometric forms. Inside the house, which also served as his office, Joe kept his collections of family portraits, porcelain,

Oriental carpets, French furniture, silk screens, and books on art and architecture. The result was warm, polished, comfortable. Joe tolerated nothing less than perfection, and a Philippine couple took care of the housekeeping under his watchful supervision. Every morning, dressed in a kimono, he eagerly discussed the day's menus with the cook before changing into one of his English suits and going into the study to review the day's schedule with his secretary, Miss Puffenberger, whom he called Puff.

In a letter of congratulations written on learning of the upcoming marriage, Marietta's twenty-year-old daughter, Frankie FitzGerald, shrewdly wondered what place Susan Mary, her godmother, would assume in Joe's clockwork existence. She even dared to slip in a prescient warning: "One thing disturbs me—and that is it may not be a practical arrangement. Can you cook? Your chefs will be so enraged when they hear about each other that they will either resign or feed you nothing but soufflés in violent, jealous competition."[7] Joe's younger brother Stewart also recommended that his future sister-in-law not let herself be dominated. He knew what he was talking about, for the two brothers had cosigned their editorials until 1958, when Stewart, wanting to be free, went his own way.

At the beginning, Joe was thrilled and determined to please. As admirable Miss Puff put it, "Mr. Alsop thinks—in fact he knows—that he invented marriage."[8] He did more than make room to accommodate the Patten family's arrival. The whole house was rearranged and expanded with a new garage (Joe did not drive, but Susan Mary did), a swimming pool, and a large bedroom for the bride. Her dresses were hung on two levels in a separate room, with a special hook to reach the top row, as at the dry cleaner's.

The marriage of Susan Mary Patten—widow of a man she had stopped loving long before he died—and Joseph Alsop—a bachelor with a double life—was celebrated at All Saints Episcopalian Church in Chevy Chase, Maryland, on February 16, 1961. Susan Mary would have preferred a small ceremony with the children in Paris, but her mother, who did not like Joe, had refused to make the trip. Joe returned to France with his wife before leaving for Laos to check on whether his domino effect theory of Communist expansion might begin in the small kingdom where a dangerous guerrilla army was running wild.

Susan Mary prepared to leave Paris, its gray walls, zinc roofs, and ever-changing skies. The city, about to be abandoned, wooed her with its prettiest accordion tunes. In autumn, a new life began. The children had to learn to speak with an American accent. Billy was at Groton and Anne went to the Potomac School. In her lovely bedroom hung with Persian blue and white wallpaper, Susan Mary tried not to dwell in a past haunted by memories. After all, as everybody was continuously and affectionately telling her, she had finally come home. Yet for years afterward, she would avoid visiting certain rooms at the National Gallery, because Impressionist paintings of the French countryside made her heart throb with sadness.

The Kennedy Years

You gave me the Kennedy years.[9]

—Susan Mary to Joe Alsop, November 3, 1976

In America, hope returns every four years. On January 20, 1961, John Fitzgerald Kennedy, standing bareheaded in the freezing cold, swore to defend the Constitution and champion freedom. "Let the word go forth from this time and place, to friend and foe alike, that the torch has been passed to a new generation of Americans." The drowsy Eisenhower years were suddenly over. Nobody knew what exactly the "New Frontier" stood for—victory over Communism, the end of poverty, the conquest of outer space? Whatever it was, the new president embodied it perfectly. The resonant tone of his address thrilled Susan Mary in Paris. The next day, Joe called to tell her that Inauguration Day, begun at the Capitol, had ended at his house. After making the round of the inaugural balls, the president had turned up on Joe's doorstep in white tie and tails, smiling, his thick, tousled hair dusted with snow. It was long past midnight and a party was still under way. The guests rose to their feet to greet him. Before the day was over, Kennedy wanted to relive it among friends. He drank a glass of champagne.

"The only problem was that there was nothing to eat in the house except left over terrapin soup which he doesn't like," Joe explained to Susan Mary.

"So what did you do?"

"I had it heated up. Thank God this time next year you will be there and able to cook up a meal on these occasions if they occur again, which I fervently hope they won't. The very last thing I want is to be known publicly as an intimate of Mr. Kennedy's as it makes my colleagues of the press furious."[10]

Of course, the next day the entire city knew about Zeus's descent from the clouds, and Joe's house passed into Washington legend, adding to its owner's glory.[11]

The meeting soon repeated itself. Two days later, Joe was invited to the first dinner given by John and Jackie in the White House. Between them, nine people consumed more than ten pounds of caviar, bemoaning all the while the ugliness of the house; Joe wailed that it was decorated like a small-town hotel. On February 14, he introduced his fiancée to the Kennedys two days before he and Susan Mary were to be married. The president loved gossip, whether from the pressroom or from London drawing rooms; Susan Mary told him about Lady Dorothy Cavendish, the wife of British prime minister Harold Macmillan, who was quietly carrying on an outrageous affair. She told the story well and made him laugh, which was one of the two things he expected from a woman. The next day, Jacqueline Kennedy sent her a friendly note saying how happy she was that they had met at last. She asked Susan Mary to call her Jackie, even though, she wrote, it was a nickname she disliked.

So it was that Joe kept the promises he had made to Susan Mary, far and above his wildest hopes. Graced with the Kennedys' favor, the Alsops figured among the star cast of an exceptional presidency. Although they did not quite belong to the innermost circle, they were regular guests at the White House, dancing the twist at cocktails and balls, dining at intimate parties of eight, six, and even four people that Jackie organized to keep her husband entertained. Pretty, witty, well-dressed Susan Mary often sat on President Kennedy's right. Her European experience also appealed to Jackie, and she was asked to join the committee in charge of finding new paintings for the White House, together with art experts and influential figures such as beautiful Babe Paley.

At the beginning of her husband's presidency, Jackie Kennedy had launched a considerable renovation project at the White House. She gathered an efficient group of people who cajoled would-be donors into generosity. Henry Francis du Pont, a great American art collector, whom Susan Mary had known since childhood, was appointed chairman. The decorator Stéphane Boudin was also called in to help, but this was kept secret because he was French and it was important not to give an impression of foreign influence. Susan Mary admired the willpower Jackie hid behind her deferential and reserved demeanor, particularly her talent for defusing tension between the oversensitive du Pont and Boudin. When du Pont did not like a particular painting, Jackie quickly had it removed, saying, "Of course you're right, Mr. du Pont." At their next lunch meeting, Susan Mary noticed that Jackie was beaming and the painting was back in its place. Her billionaire adviser did not dare say a thing.

Besides historic furniture, the art committee acquired five hundred paintings and engravings. By the end of the year, the White House had been transformed. On January 15, 1962, CBS made a documentary about the restoration with Jackie leading the tour. That evening, some of the rushes of the seven-hour session were shown to the Kennedys and close friends, the Alsops among them. Everybody congratulated Jackie. Exhausted, hair down, sipping on her scotch, she savored the praise from her husband, who had disliked his own performance on screen.

The Kennedys also willingly accepted invitations to dine at Dumbarton Avenue. These were evenings during which Anne had to give up her bedroom to Secret Service officers. Jackie sensed that Joe admired her, and felt she could talk to him about everything that interested her, meaning anything but politics. The president knew he would be given good French wines and meet interesting or amusing guests, often pretty and well-born English women. In December 1961 he dined in the company of the Duchess of Devonshire, who was a great friend of his. He also met Diana Cooper in February 1963. "What a woman!" he exclaimed, thoroughly charmed by the septuagenarian. In June of the same year, he invited himself over to the Alsops' house while Jackie was away in the country. He had just made an important speech on American-Soviet relations, but he turned the conversation to the Profumo affair, a spicy London cocktail of sex, politics, and espionage. He chatted with Mary Meyer, his current mistress, and flirted for a long while with young Antonia Fraser. Sir Maurice Bowra, former vice-chancellor of Oxford, was furious to receive only thirty seconds of presidential attention. As Joe later told his friend Evangeline Bruce, Kennedy looked that evening "rather like a small boy wondering whether to plunge a spoon into a fresh dish of peach ice cream."[12]

Although Susan Mary was not as intimate with the presidential couple as her husband was and viewed every dinner as a hurdle to be cleared, the close relationship with the Kennedys pleased her as much as it did Joe. She would never have admitted to pride, however, and merely said how grateful she was to be able, from time to time, to take the president's mind off his heavy responsibilities. John Kennedy probably never tried to seduce Susan Mary—too proper and starched—but he was friendly and attentive. Both loved history, particularly dramatic events and remarkable figures. "You were very good this evening," said Joe, satisfied by his wife's success, "but stop talking only about serious matters and David Cecil's books. Tell him who's sleeping with whom, he loves that." Neither Joe nor Susan Mary had the faintest inkling about Kennedy's secret life.

One evening was special. On October 16, 1962,[13] the Alsops had organized a farewell dinner for Avis and Chip Bohlen, who had just been appointed ambassador to France. The Grahams and Isaiah Berlin had been invited as well as Hervé Alphand, the French ambassador (in spite of Joe's grumbling). It was a mild evening. Kennedy and Chip strolled and chatted beneath the magnolia trees for so long that the lamb went cold. When the president finally came to the table, Susan Mary felt she was sitting next to a motor running at full speed. He was exceptionally energetic, yet he kept his usual calm and controlled voice as he repeatedly asked Bohlen and Berlin how Russians behave when they are cornered.

"Something is going on," said Susan Mary to Joe on her way to bed.

"You think so? Good night, darling. It was a great party."

She was right. That very morning the president had been shown aerial photographs of Cuba, which proved that the Soviets, contrary to their denials, were installing missile bases within striking distance of the United States. The worst crisis of the cold war was about to begin.

The Alsops were also friendly with the president's men. Kennedy had attracted people from various social backgrounds, political affiliations, and areas of expertise who shared a love for their leader and a taste for action. They were often academics, intellectuals who enjoyed exerting power. They had their sights fixed on China and the Soviet Union, and although they knew that nuclear apocalypse could strike at any moment, the threat of annihilation only added to the thrill of the job. Hardened by the Second World War in which they had served under the generals they were now shunting into retirement, they dreamed of defeating international Communism, a menace that seemed to lie in wait everywhere they turned. Like Kennedy, these cowboys of the atomic age worked hard and played harder. The ones closest to Joe were the national security adviser, McGeorge Bundy; Bundy's second in command, Walt W. Rostow; the president's brother-in-law, Sargeant Shriver; and Lawrence O'Brien, a political mastermind who handled relations with Congress. There was also Arthur Schlesinger, an old friend of Joe's whom Kennedy had stolen away from Adlai Stevenson and Harvard and entrusted with an undefined and glamorous job at the White House.

Joe and Susan Mary also often saw Bobby and Ethel Kennedy. While Susan Mary certainly raised an eyebrow at facetious Ethel, who was known to have pushed a fully clothed guest into the swimming pool, she admired the struggle against segregation that Bobby led as attorney general. In June 1963, the Alsops spent an evening with Bobby aboard the presidential yacht, the *Honey Fitz*, where Susan Mary met Nicholas Katzenbach, Bobby's deputy, a man she immediately liked.

"Tell me about what happened the other day with Wallace," she said.

"Are you sure you really want to know?"[14]

Because she insisted, he told her how he had stood up to Governor George Wallace, who had physically blocked two black students from entering the University of Alabama. The confrontation had been caught on film. After seeing the clip on June 11, the president followed Bobby's advice and gave a televised speech on civil rights the same evening. Susan Mary found the speech excellent, and hoped that the antisegregation law proposed by the president would make it through Congress. She also kept informed on the issue through leaders of the black community, like Martin Luther King Jr., who came to Dumbarton Avenue that summer—one marked by a wave of riots and demonstrations. On August 28, she watched King's "I Have a Dream" speech on television and thought it equal to Lincoln's Gettysburg Address.

The 1960s were Georgetown's glory years. Ever since the New Deal, Washington's oldest neighborhood had been the center of American power and the seat of an intellectual and social elite that had chosen to serve the nation. Diplomats, politicians, journalists, senior CIA officials: they all had attended the same schools and universities and had enlisted to fight in the cold war. In spite of their anti-Communist views, they were opposed to McCarthy's methods and demagoguery. They formed a friendly network with its own rituals: Sunday night suppers, dance classes, and, during the early postwar years, cooking classes for the women and Joe. Together, they brunched and played tennis, drank cocktails and spent weekends in the country: social life was but an extension of work. Politics, particularly foreign policy, was the only real subject of conversation, and it was analyzed and picked apart around the dinner table, accompanied by side dishes of jokes, anecdotes, gossip, and speculation. Joe loved getting into arguments and could be depended on to shout down his opponents. After dinner, he would take the men to the garden room for brandy and cigars. Leaning forward, elbows on knees, he would listen for a while, then jump in. "What are we going to do about the massive increase of the Russian arsenal?" He would clear his throat and launch into a speech while the ash from his cigarette fell unheeded to the marble floor.

Susan Mary had no trouble fitting into this patrician world, which felt passionate about the public good. She may have seemed exotic, with her Parisian air and unremitting elegance, but she liked walking at a fast pace and winning at tennis, and she understood that parties were the evening side of political life. She knew the job; she was a Jay by birth and an Alsop by marriage—she took a prominent place in the firmament and remained there to the end.

During the gilded Kennedy era, Joe and Susan Mary's circle grew remarkably in influence and prestige. "What does Georgetown think?" the White House had taken to asking. Although some friends, like Frank Wisner and Dick Bissell, stopped working for the CIA, the former for health reasons and the latter because he was deemed responsible for the disastrous Bay of Pigs invasion in April 1961, others had taken important jobs in diplomacy or advising the president. This was the case with Dean Acheson, Chip Bohlen, Paul Nitze, and Averell Harriman. Journalist friends included Phil Graham, Joseph

Kraft, and the attractive Ben Bradlee. It was a good time to be a journalist. Unlike Eisenhower, Kennedy liked the press and had told his staff to give easy access.

All of Joe's wishes seemed to be coming true. Thanks to his social standing and Roosevelt connections, he had always been close to power, which he usually respected, not out of awe but because its goals seemed noble. In his view, the position he held was beneficial to his work. Readers could be sure that his facts— he prided himself on offering facts, not mere commentary—came from the best sources. Under Kennedy, Joe felt he had truly entered the engine room of American politics. From the 1960 election onward, he was asked for advice on cabinet appointments. Even though Dean Rusk would get the job of secretary of state over Joe's candidate, David Bruce, Joe still had the impression that he had been responsible for Douglas Dillon's appointment as secretary of the Treasury. A friendly rapport developed between Joe and his president. Crises were happening all the time, and this made things all the more exciting. The president would confide in Joe, hinting at the difficulties of his June 1961 meeting with Khrushchev in Vienna or at his stormy relationship with the French president. They would discuss the matter and Joe would give Kennedy his point of view. "Mr. President, you've got to understand, independence is like a religion to General de Gaulle." After going on assignment abroad, Joe would report to the White House. In the fall of 1963, just back from Saigon, he spoke at length of the need to make changes to Ngo Dinh Diem's government. Kennedy patiently listened to Joe's tirades and fiery exhortations because he appreciated his friend's discretion and absolute loyalty.

However special, Kennedy's treatment of Joe was not unique. Other important columnists, like Walter Lippman, thought by many to be the greatest of all, or the *New York Times'* James Reston, were also courted and consulted by the president. These connections helped neutralize criticism, amplify successes, and facilitate leaks. Nobody seemed to mind the symbiotic relationship the presidency had with the press. All the same, Joe's brother Stewart had chosen to keep his distance in hopes of maintaining, as he put it, a clearer judgment.

Two weeks before the trip to Texas in November 1963, Joe and Susan Mary dined at the Kennedy White House for the last time. The president asked his wife to show their friends the pink suit she was planning to wear in Dallas. Joe and Susan Mary wished them luck. Visiting a Southern state would be no easy task for a president who had shown support for civil rights.

On the cold gray afternoon of Friday, November 22, 1963, Susan Mary was lunching alone in her study because Joe had a guest. Being kept away was an unpleasant but inevitable situation to which she had grown accustomed. There was a knock on her door. "Come quick. Somebody shot the president!" She hurried to the radio and heard the news. Joe had to be told.

Joe sat, still and silent, alone in his little sitting room. The telephone kept ringing. Susan Mary picked it up. It was Jock Whitney, the owner of the *New York Herald Tribune,* begging Joe to write a piece. "Tell him I can't. I don't have anything to say," whispered Joe. John Kenneth Galbraith came after dinner and told them with great feeling that none of Kennedy's team wanted to work for Johnson. Finally, in the middle of the night, Joe managed to write a farewell column titled "Go, Stranger!" He and Susan Mary spent Saturday at the White House, Susan Mary lending a hand where she could and Joe trying to convince his friends to stay on with the new president. On Sunday night, Jackie called Susan Mary, making sure that the invitations for the funeral Mass the next day had arrived. Joe took the telephone and suggested she come and live with them until a new house was found. This made Jackie regain her normal voice for a moment and almost laugh. "Joe, dear Joe, do you realize that the children and I have nine dogs between us?"[15] The ceremony was held on Monday morning at Saint Matthew's Cathedral. Susan Mary would always remember Joe's terrible silence and the look on Bobby Kennedy's face.

"I had no idea that I loved him," wrote Joe years later. "I don't go in for loving men. But nothing in my life has moved me as it did, not even the death of my father. And everyone has said the same. As though he were the one thing we most valued and could never replace."[16]

"Yes, you're right, it's been hardest on the men," wrote Susan Mary to Avis Bohlen.[17] Always wanting to make herself useful, she spent long weeks in the basement of the Old State Department with her sister-in-law Tish Alsop and a group of diplomats' wives, answering thousands of letters of condolence that flooded in from all over the world.

Quagmire

In the end, Joe's friends Bundy, Dillon, McNamara, and Salinger all decided to serve the new president, a man they had politely ignored during the years he had been, in title, second in command.

Joe knew Johnson as a matter of course, and immediately sent a letter expressing his trust and support. On Monday, November 25, he called him on the telephone. Both men were versed in the art of flattery and manipulation and wanted to come to an understanding that would benefit America's best interests.

So it was that Joe and Susan Mary continued to go to the White House. In May 1964, Susan Mary was invited to tea with a group of people from the artistic world. Mrs. Johnson was wearing her prettiest afternoon dress and wanted to show that she was capable of following in Jackie Kennedy's footsteps. Still, the style had changed, becoming "most curious and interesting."[18] "They entertain in a warm, Texan way," recounted Susan Mary after dining with the Johnsons. "I'm growing rather fond of Ladybird, but what about those macabre daughters, Lucybird and Lindabird? They generally wear sequined black slacks and slip up to one just as Mac Bundy is beginning to spill the beans about something interesting, twist one's ear, and say 'You're right cute, Mrs. Alsop, want to hear what my English teacher said today?'"[19] Another time, the president of the United States pinched her behind and exclaimed for all to hear, "Why does such a thin girl wear a garter belt?"[20]

In June, the Alsops dined with the Johnsons and their close friends Clark Clifford, Jack Valenti, and their wives. It was a pleasant evening—the heavy summer humidity had not set in yet—so they took a stroll on the South Lawn. Susan Mary noticed a black suitcase the size of a large radio being carried around by two strapping secret security officers and wondered with curiosity if it was *the* button. A hundred feet away, the men were discussing Vietnam.

Joe's opinion on Vietnam was in line with his beliefs about the global war against Communism. He felt America had obligations toward South Vietnam, a small, fragile state deserving foreign assistance. He also felt strongly about the danger of Communism spreading in Southeast Asia, all the more as China had already fallen in 1949. At the time, Joe had criticized the United States for letting China go, and now, according to him, the situation in Vietnam required vigorous action. It was a matter of honor and prestige, not to mention America's position in Asia and the world in general. Joe had returned from Vietnam in May 1964 and sounded a rallying cry, but it was an election year, and Johnson did not want to show his hand or be pushed into engagement. In December, Joe went back to Saigon and became even more alarmed. He started making comparisons to Kennedy's behavior during the Cuban Missile Crisis, which annoyed the president. For Joe, the stakes and the solution were the same as they had been in Cuba: America had to deploy force and use it, if necessary. Courage and virility were called for. Cunningly, Joe played on Johnson's fear of appearing weak in the eyes of history, and his loud editorials maintained pressure.

Joe's access to the White House was gradually reduced, but to his credit, this did nothing to change his convictions. All that mattered were the results of his persistent hammering. In the spring of 1965, the decisions he had been vehemently demanding began to be made. On February 13, Johnson ordered the bombing of a North Vietnamese military camp; a few weeks later, he granted General Westmoreland's request and sent two battalions of marines to Vietnam on a security mission to protect the Da Nang Air Base. American military involvement in the region quickly escalated. On July 28, the president held a press conference to announce that he would raise the number of combat troops in Vietnam to 120,000 men. It was much less than what the general staff was asking for, but they would soon be getting nearly all the recruits they wanted.

For the entire length of the war, one that was never formally declared, the field officers in Saigon had Joe on their side. From 1965 to 1972 he made one or two trips a year to Vietnam. "General Alsop," as the president called him when he was feeling charitable, received VIP treatment, staying with the ambassador or at the Hotel Majestic. From these bases, he descended on his prey—diplomats, military men, and other journalists—and went into the field. While his detractors disapproved of his modus operandi, the means of transport that were made available to him (planes, helicopters, jeeps), and his privileged access, they never attacked his courage and endurance. High on the heady fumes of war's grit and fraternity, Joe relived his war days in China and Korea. He liked staying in Saigon, where the service was impeccable and the evenings on the colonial terraces so pleasant. He admired the generals, found the soldiers intrepid, and called the young university graduates who were working to pacify the locals, such as Frank Wisner, the son of his friends Frank and Polly, the new Lawrences of Arabia. In contrast to these heroes, he viewed the young journalists who dared challenge the army's reports as despicable miscreants. In his eyes they were either stupid or unpatriotic, and, in any case, off-limits.

Lined up like the payload of a B-52 bomber, his editorials fell hard on Washington. They seemed more bent on convincing readers than informing them. Targeting a president who Joe wished were more resolute, they effectively rephrased Westmoreland and DePuy's military bulletins into catchy one-liners. According to Joe, the United States was on the verge of victory, it just needed to make a last effort; the enemy was overwhelmed by the superior moral and military force of the American army; every North Vietnamese attack was the last; a light was shining at the end of the tunnel.

This raging optimism had a shrinking audience in a country that still supported the war effort but where opposition was growing on college campuses and in important newspapers, such as the *New York Times*. Without being as categorical as Joe, Susan Mary still believed that the war could be won and that . America did not have the right to let South Vietnam down. But she also listened to the dissenting voices who spoke in favor of negotiations, like that of their friend Senator John Sherman Cooper. She closely followed the February 1966 televised hearings held by J. William Fulbright, the chairman of the Senate Committee on Foreign Relations. Still, Joe's rants drowned out Susan Mary's murmured and nuanced observations. He roared at what he took to be a betrayal by the intellectual elite, not even sparing his friends Arthur Schlesinger and Bobby Kennedy when he saw their positions begin to waver. In June 1967, the Six-Day War brought an intermission to Joe's obsession. "The heaven of not talking about Vietnam night after night," wrote a weary Susan Mary in a letter to Marietta. "Now that the Middle East smoulders instead of flaming, I suppose we will be back floundering in that poisonous bog that seems to infect the healthiest conversation as dangerously as a tropical fever."[21]

The Tet Offensive at the end of January 1968 was a brutal wake-up call. America was appalled to discover the power of the enemy. Mistakenly thought to be at bay, the North Vietnamese had come out of the jungle to strike urban targets, forcing Ambassador Ellsworth Bunker to flee the residence in his pajamas. A month later, Walter Cronkite declared in an editorial report on CBS that the United States was at an impasse. The only way out was to negotiate with Hanoi. A defeated President Johnson, who had once hoped to realize his Great Society reforms, announced he would not run for reelection.

It was a dark year for Joe Alsop. The nation was undergoing a social and cultural shift that upended the values, principles, and institutions he held dear. America's youth was calling the war in Vietnam immoral, rejecting authority, and spitting on the flag. Even girls from good families, like Frankie FitzGerald and Elizabeth Alsop, Stewart's daughter, were swept up in the movement. The assassination of Martin Luther King Jr. unleashed the violence King had managed to keep under control; Bobby Kennedy's subsequent death, which badly traumatized Joe, broke apart the Democratic Party and allowed Nixon, that phoenix of American politics, to take the presidential election in November. Joe's friends Bundy and McNamara had thrown in the towel long before, and Joe now felt he was carrying the cause for the war in Vietnam on his own. He became the object of a polemic, with articles in the *New Republic* and *Harper's* denouncing his political positions, mannerisms, and eccentricity.

Isolated and ridiculed, Joe refused to surrender and fought back blow for blow. The war was his life. He wasn't discouraged by bad news from the front; it only stirred up his pugnacious nature. His columns were no longer a sufficient outlet for the fury that welled inside him, ready to pour out at any moment at the slightest provocation. Nobody was safe, apart from Billy and Anne, whom he adored. Friends remained faithful, but they came to dread his dinner parties. When his temper flared too high, Susan Mary would intervene, "Come Joe, calm down." Then he would lash out, rough and insulting, and she knew she was beaten.

VIII

Anatomy of a Marriage

It's Worth It

*And you know, Avis, looking at the elephant grey lives of
so many of the friends we both were brought up with, cela
vaut la peine.*[1]

—Letter from Susan Mary to Avis Bohlen, October 1968

Life with Joe had ups and downs. When her husband was in a
good mood, Susan Mary counted her blessings. The children got
along well with their generous and attentive stepfather, who had
helped them adapt to America. He supervised their studies (Anne
was now in middle school and Billy was at Harvard) and showered
them with gifts and advice. He encouraged them in their first
romantic relationships and tolerated their adolescent awkwardness
better than their mother did. Joe also brought Susan Mary
financial security, taking care of her and planning for her future.
She enjoyed being part of the welcoming Alsop clan and liked her
comfortable house. Her friend the French diplomat Bobby de

Margerie approvingly said it was starting to look as though a Noailles lived there. Her chaste companionship with Joe did not bother her; it was compensated by privileges like regularly playing hostess to a brilliant cast of characters such as Ted Heath, I. M. Pei, Zbigniew Brzezinski, Moshe Dayan, and George Cukor. Although she did not care much for big receptions, she liked embassy parties and made it to New York to attend the dinner given by Marietta before Truman Capote's Black and White Ball.

Still, Joe was the boss. Experienced though she was in social matters, she agreed to this and had quietly given up the idea that she might help him with his work. Susan Mary came from a generation whose intelligent women gracefully accepted their place as satellites orbiting masculine suns. In the perfunctory role that was left to her, she expected little praise from her husband—and hardly got any.

Joe's impertinence often made Susan Mary laugh. She felt protected by his unwavering self-confidence. One evening in December 1964, after the American film premiere of *My Fair Lady*, Joe refused to take the bus that was supposed to drive him and other guests to the British Embassy. Spying a limousine, he and his friend Marella Agnelli got in. Another couple was already sitting inside.

"Did you like the film?" Joe asked the strangers. "I didn't. It's not really good."

"You're quite right. It was lousy," said the smiling young woman. She wore her dark brown hair in a chignon and a white silk evening gown by Givenchy.

On their way to the embassy, Joe listed the film's shortcomings to its leading lady, Audrey Hepburn, and her husband, Mel

Ferrer. "What can I say, I just didn't recognize her," Joe explained later. "But she agreed with me."[2]

Not everything was so funny. Joe was often rude to his wife, interrupting and criticizing her in public. Anything could set him off: a dinner menu, a seating arrangement, a missing cushion, or merely a remark he felt was too banal or superficial. Whenever he drank too much he lost his temper, shouted, and raved, veering out of control; Susan Mary would go silent, looking like a virgin martyr. Sometimes, though, she struggled and tried to justify herself with the clumsy and voluble insistence of those who know they are doomed. Neither attitude did her any good. Whether she chose to be submissive or fight back, Joe remained equally exasperated.

Indifference or sheer anger might have served Susan Mary better in her arguments with Joe, but she was inexperienced in wielding such weapons. Instead, she would attempt to vindicate her husband's behavior: he was overworked, or it was the situation in Vietnam. She never complained, but she withdrew within herself like an elegant woman, caught up in a crowd, clutches her skirts about her for fear of being knocked into. Her face hardened and her hair, blown back in a rigid bouffant, seemed as though it were cut from a single block of dark stone, each lock held tightly in place.

She never complained, not even to her closest friends, merely hinting at marital problems. Only Billy and her brother-in-law Stewart Alsop sometimes heard the truth. Often she just fled. She would spend February in Marietta's Palladian mansion in Barbados, or she would go to Maine, or, better still, to Europe, Italy, London, Paris. Taking refuge on the old Continent, she felt at home and breathed more easily. Her many friends doted on her—"balm to the ego"[3]—and she could play her favorite role, that of an American woman civilized to the tips of her Vivier-shod toes. During the spring of 1969, Stewart Alsop knew Susan Mary was feeling particularly low, so he and Tom Braden, a journalist and close friend, took her traveling. She admired the crocuses in London, passed through Paris, and had a shopping spree at Balmain before going to Cairo and visiting the archaeological site of Petra in Jordan. Joe wrote her a check for expenses and gave her introductions. He thought her letters home were marvelous.

All things considered, Susan Mary hoped she could hold out. She did not want a divorce. From time to time, Joe would bring up the idea of a separation, not as a threat but as a solution to their uneasy daily life. As he told his friend Kay Graham, he had begun to feel constrained and trapped after the first euphoric months of marriage. Living with someone requires adjusting to the person's rhythms and moods, and even with separate bedrooms, this turned out to be more difficult than he had imagined. He was still proud of his wife—always telling Billy his mother was the prettiest woman at the parties they went to—but she frequently irritated him and he was not used to holding his tongue about what he felt.

Joe and Susan Mary often wrote to each other, leaving little notes around the house, especially when locked in a quarrel. In them, Susan Mary replied to Joe's questions about their future, severely judging her weaknesses and faults: "I'm very bossy, and possessive, and tiresome."[4] Deploring her lack of energy, she noted, "It's a tragedy that I don't have the vitality that a wife

should have to 'keep up' to the very gay *va-et-vient* of this house."[5]
Emphasizing her progress, she made resolutions: "I'm going to try
immensely hard to give up any efforts to change you."[6] With an
unfeigned humility that, given the circumstances, might seem
excessive, she opened up her heart: "I have a feeling that I'm really
not much good at marriage, I am perhaps meant to be a friend or
a mother, roles that I think I can play, and I feel terribly sorry for
anyone who has to put up with me steadily. However I do so miss
you when you aren't around that the thought of a life without you
seems to me unbearable. You are right to suggest separating if
things don't go this year, but I know that I should hate it, and I
pray for self-discipline so that you will be spared scenes. Whatever
happens, it's important for you to remember how much you have
given me. I love you more than anyone I have known and I've
loved quite a lot."[7] The word *love* was repeated with pitiful and
trembling conviction. In a letter written after a stay in Maine in
July 1969 during which Billy celebrated his twenty-first birthday
and made a toast to his mother of "immense charm,"[8] she
reaffirmed her commitment: "Yes, darling, I would like to
continue to try to make a go of it."[9]

Nixon, Kissinger, and China

After a long flight during which Susan Mary read Gabriel García
Márquez's *One Hundred Years of Solitude*, which had been a gift
from Billy, she landed in Hong Kong under a misty rain that
blurred the outlines of the city's skyscrapers. The next day she and
Joe were in Saigon, where the temperature was ninety degrees in
the shade.

"The American presence has not the shrill loud stridency of our presence in Europe in the war and post war—it's so low key that one almost feels that the French are still here, for the town is still a tropical copy of Arles or Nîmes—no Roman ruins, but even the same trees, their seed brought from France years ago, Byrrh and Dubonnet signs fly flecked and dusty, la grande place, la mairie—pâtisserie baroque in architecture, le Cercle Hippique, le Cercle Sportif."[10]

She and Joe stayed in a villa that was "probably built by the assistant vice-president of the Banque de l'Indochine about 1900."[11] The city was off-limits to military personnel and there was not a single GI in sight, but the local officials were welcoming and relaxed. Susan Mary spent time with her cousin Charlie Whitehouse, who was in charge of pacifying the surrounding provinces. She played tennis early in the morning before the heat of the day and explored the city in the American ambassador's Ford, which seemed shabby when compared to the British ambassador's Rolls-Royce, but was armored and equipped with an automatic rifle, as she discovered when a bomb exploded in the street. In spite of this, she refused to wear a bulletproof vest, saying, "too hot, I preferred to die."[12] For months, she had been looking forward to seeing Angkor Wat, but the trip was ultimately canceled because the United States was preparing to send troops into Cambodia in March 1970. "*Tant pis,* I'm off to Northern Thailand, said to be very pretty."[13]

Although she enjoyed visiting new places, Susan Mary was no ordinary tourist. Back in Washington, she let it be known that she had been favorably impressed by American action on the ground in Vietnam, an opinion that was repeated in high places.

However hostile he was to the press and ill at ease with Georgetown society, President Nixon cultivated Joe's support of the war and knew about Susan Mary. On May 8, 1970, he sent her a note. "Your encouragements for our country's goal in Southeast Asia mean a great deal to America's fighting men as well as to me. I was pleased to hear from you and I want you to know how much your comments are appreciated."[14] She did not think the Republican president a very appealing man, but the letter was flattering.

While Susan Mary was extremely grateful to Joe for the trip and knew what she owed him—"all my historic moments have been with you"[15]—she still had to endure the continuing unpleasantness that resulted from her husband's passionate commitment to the Vietnam War. At the beginning of 1970, the humorist and *Washington Post* columnist Art Buchwald had a play on Broadway called *Sheep on the Runway*. It told the story of an American journalist's disastrous visit to Nonomura, an imaginary principality near the Chinese border. When the journalist, Joe Mayflower, wrongly perceives a Communist threat from the inoffensive rebellion brewing in the north of Nonomura, he sounds the alarm in Washington. In less than no time, the peaceful country is wracked with fire and bathed in blood.

> JOE: Stop shaking your head at me. I've come halfway round the world to see you. I could have been with Pompidou. I could have been with Tito. I come here to tell you there's a threat to your little country and you keep shaking your head at me. I won't have it. There are people all over the world begging me for the benefit of

my wisdom and my advice. And, you sit there and shake your head at me. Charles de Gaulle never shook his head at me. Lyndon Johnson never shook his head at me. No one has ever done that to me.

PRINCE: Please, please, Mr. Mayflower. All right, all right. What do you want me to say?

JOE: I want you to recognize that there is a threat out there.

PRINCE: All right, all right, there's a threat, there's a threat.

JOE: *(Calm and dignified)* That's very interesting, Your Highness. Though it doesn't surprise me. *(Takes out pad)* When did you first become aware of this danger?

PRINCE: Well . . . how about . . . last Wednesday? [16]

Art Buchwald could protest all he liked, everybody knew that Joe Mayflower was Joe Alsop. Joe took it very badly, considered suing Buchwald, and forbade his friends from seeing the play. Stewart flew to his brother's rescue, but most of Washington just chose sides and was highly amused. There were other distasteful happenings. One Sunday in November, obscene drawings referring to Joe were made on a car parked in front of a church in their neighborhood. "A ridiculous little episode," [17] said Susan Mary dismissively, supporting her husband without ever alluding to his sexuality. Then she found hurtful words about Joe on her own car. Things got even worse when the compromising photos of Joe taken in Moscow in 1957 resurfaced and began circulating through town, probably at the initiative of Soviet agents. Fortunately, everybody remained calm and the incident stopped there.

In spite of these worries, the year ended on a positive note.

Billy (now known as Bill) married Kate Bacon in Boston on December 19. Kate's mother, lovely Kitty, was the youngest of Susan Mary's cousins. It was a family marriage prepared by the two mothers and by Joe, who went to a lot of trouble because he loved his stepson and wanted things to be done properly. Two years earlier he had been similarly involved in Anne's wedding to George Crile, the son of a good family from Cleveland. "It is odd for a man who has never had children of his own to enjoy being a father and to long to be a grandfather," Joe Alsop wrote to one of his friends.[18] Susan Mary also remarked on this enthusiasm, but with a touch of acidity: "Joe sees romance in the touching way that childless people often do."[19] Because she thought her daughter was too young to be getting married—pretty Anne had just turned eighteen—she had tried to delay the event, behaving, she said in a letter to Marietta, "like the Eastern dowager in a high dog collar."[20] She did not protest with much conviction, though, and the marriage took place on September 21, 1968, the date originally decided on by the young couple. Anne and George moved to the West Coast, where Susan Mary was happy to go and visit them. Barefoot in the California sunshine, she felt, for a short, blessed moment, that she was no longer proper Mrs. Alsop.

Susan Mary liked speed, especially behind the wheel. She hated waiting and easily grew impatient. Although new things interested her, at the end of the 1960s the world seemed to be changing at a dizzying pace. As soon as she got used to the idea of rock and roll being played at elegant dinner dances, Bob Dylan replaced Elvis Presley. After Courrèges, she thought hemlines would remain high, but once she had her skirts tailored, she discovered that Saint Laurent was lengthening them again and even making flowing ankle-length dresses. What was one to do? Luckily, being thin never seemed to go out of fashion. In New York, she had to give up an old favorite, the red-and-gold opera house, and become acquainted with the new Metropolitan Opera, which had been built as part of Lincoln Center. There were also unknown faces at parties. "Very clever or very pretty people who have nothing to do with New York society as it was when I was young. Rather more fun on the whole—not a fine old name in the lot."[21] But Susan Mary remained intrepid. In January 1972, she treated herself to a little plastic surgery. It pleased Joe and she happily reported to her son, "Everyone should have their faces lifted, it's morale building."[22] She went to see the new shows, such as the film *Alice's Restaurant* and the musical *Jesus Christ Superstar*, with the Margeries and their son Gilles. During the musical, the audience whistled in disapproval when they heard the actors recite classic, respected texts. "I thought that Jesus, Lincoln, and Martin Luther King were still OK—clearly I was wrong. Back to school."[23]

An age was passing. Joe's mother, always warm and loving with Susan Mary, died in June 1971. Stewart was hospitalized for a harmless problem that turned out to be leukemia. Bravely, he battled the disease to the end, going through repeated stays in clinics and transfusions for which Joe often donated his own blood. Mrs. Jay had also grown weaker, suffering strokes in 1967 and 1969 that hampered her autonomy without dampening her severity. Powerless, she remained imperious and demanding, with brief moments of sentimentality that made her cling to her daughter. Old Mrs. Jay was very fond of Anne and happy about the birth of Bill's son, Sam, her great-grandson, in the summer of

1971. The baby spent the first few months of his life at Dumbarton Avenue.

There were also upheavals in foreign politics. Faced with the difficult task of pulling America out of Vietnam, Nixon, assisted by his national security adviser, Henry Kissinger, was pursuing negotiations begun in Paris, while continuing to use force on the ground. The offensive side of this strategy pleased Joe, who was moreover very supportive of Kissinger, a figure he had immediately recognized and adopted as one of his own. A Washington newcomer in 1969, Kissinger was a Harvard professor who had become the darling of Georgetown and a close friend to Joe and Susan Mary.

On February 7, 1971, preparations for the Alsops' usual Sunday dinner for twenty-four were already under way when the president called and recommended that Joe turn on the television at ten in the evening. Kay Graham, who was single-handedly running the *Washington Post* empire since the death of her husband, went into Susan Mary's bedroom to call her team. Kissinger had barely arrived for dinner when the phone started ringing. He received eleven calls over the course of the evening, with an impressed but annoyed Susan Mary serving as his switchboard operator. At ten o'clock, the guests gathered around the television, but there was no White House speech, only a short announcement from the South Vietnamese president, Nguyen Van Thieu.

"Why on earth did he call us?" Joe asked Susan Mary. "We look like awful fools."

"That's Washington for you. How is one to interpret a President's thinking?"[24]

The next day, South Vietnamese troops began invading Laos

in hopes of cutting supply lines to North Vietnam. The operation reawakened violent antiwar protests in the United States.

The ongoing war in Vietnam did not prevent Nixon and Kissinger from seeking détente with China and the Soviet Union. On July 18, 1971, Kissinger came to see the Alsops on his return from a secret trip to Beijing, where he had met with Zhou Enlai. It was the first time in almost twenty-five years that American and Chinese officials had come into contact. That evening, the atmosphere at Dumbarton Avenue was positively electric. An excellent storyteller, Kissinger outdid himself, and although he did not go into the substance of the talks, what little he told was highly interesting.

The following spring, the Nixons had a small reception for the eighty-eighth birthday of Alice Roosevelt Longworth, Joe's impertinent cousin, who was feared and revered by all of Washington. Over drinks, Susan Mary chatted with a particularly warm and relaxed president. He told her about his recent meeting with Mao, whom he found physically exhausted but intellectually alert. Their conversation continued at dinner. Joe, who approved of the opening of relations with China so as better to confound the Soviet Union, was nevertheless worried about America's gullibility concerning Chinese leaders. Piqued, Kissinger tried to reassure him.

"We trust none of them," Kissinger said.

"Nor do they we but they have had a chance to sum us up, judge us, have some sort of idea of how we think, our pattern of thought," said Nixon. "Surely this is useful?"

"It's not just useful," declared Joe, more Mayflower than ever, "it's tremendously important."[25]

In November 1972, the Alsops made their own journey to Beijing. Susan Mary had been studying and could recite all the Chinese dynasties by heart.

"This *is* the trip of my life."[26] It was almost an official voyage, and it included a meeting with the Chinese prime minister. From half past nine in the evening until one in the morning, Joe listened to Zhou Enlai talk about birth control, agricultural production, and Leonid Brezhnev, whom Zhou found even more fearsome than Khrushchev. Seated next to the two men in the huge reception hall, Susan Mary took notes.

"Is there anything I can do for you during your visit, Mr. Alsop?" asked Zhou at the end of the conversation.

"There is, Sir. I would like to take my wife traveling into the interior."

"Where?"

"To Yunnan and Szechwan. Would that be impossible?"

"Not at all. When would you like to go? Would three o'clock suit you?"[27]

At the appointed time, they boarded a military plane. Resplendent in his brand-new red fox fur hat, Joe revisited the places he had flown across thirty years earlier with General Chennault. But Susan Mary's favorite memory remained the Forbidden City.

"There were tall willows, water and two old musicians playing their instruments against the walls, because the sound, the resonance is better that way. It was haunting, just a moment of old China. Silence, but for the musicians. Then noise, interpreters, all that, but we noticed the moment, and loved it."[28]

The Breakup

Devotion is not always disinterested. It can help fight boredom, build up credit, or even serve as subtle revenge upon a person whose ascendancy is reduced by age or sickness. None of this applied to Susan Mary. Her upbringing had left her with a sharp sense of responsibility, "a noble child of Duty," Joe used to say, raising his eyes to heaven. Susan Mary liked to think this was the driving force behind her actions, and perhaps it was. Taking care of her mother seemed as necessary and normal as writing to the elderly woman in France who had looked after her children, or visiting the sick at Washington's General Hospital, something she had done for years. Susan Mary liked being of use—she would lend a dress or connect people with such rapidity that those she helped hardly realized it. Her children had always been the first objects of her attention, often financial in form. In fact, where they were concerned, generosity came more naturally to her than an open ear. It was through letters and presents that she showed her love.

But the full measure of Susan Mary's talents unfolded when duty crossed paths with friendship. She could be silent when it was fitting, full of sensible advice and resolute when needed. This happened in July 1965, when she stayed at Marietta's side in London after the death of her cherished Adlai Stevenson, and in August 1972, when she delayed her return to the United States to be in France with Elise Bordeaux-Groult, whose asthma and nervous fatigue had got the better of her. A year later, Elise's suffering grew worse and Susan Mary flew to France again, trying to stand between her sick friend and the inevitable. On June 27, Elise died in the American Hospital. A few days later, her family and friends dined together on the Rue du Bac. The evening had begun normally, as Marina Sulzberger recounted. Then "one by one they broke down. Susan Mary a rock. She is fabulous. But all of us undone."[29]

During the following summer, walking through the pine forests of Northeast Harbor, Susan Mary came to a decision, the most agonizing of her life. Had Elise's death made her more aware of the passage of time? Had Joe uttered one cruel word too many? She realized that he would not change, and that if she did nothing, she would eventually fall apart. She had to protect herself. As it was, she lived in fear and felt herself shrinking under her husband's harsh criticism. Her self-esteem, not strong at best, was relentlessly shaken, and her insecurity grew as, unsuccessfully, she tried to fend off attacks that left her dispirited and full of doubts. Strong emotions had never appealed to her; she preferred them watered down with gentle banter. Instead, she was caught up in continual and exhausting confrontations that she made worse by playing them over and over in her head. In addition to the suffering caused by her marriage, she found herself forced into a state of perpetual self-analysis, an exercise she disliked as she equated it with self-indulgence.

"I really do think that we are lovers, otherwise we wouldn't be so miserable about hurting each other."[30] This heartrending admission, made a few years earlier, still held true, but Susan Mary was no longer content with such tortured satisfaction. She hated fuss, so she left quietly. The *Washington Star* of September

26, 1973, published a brief announcement noting the separation. Susan Mary soberly declared that she was grateful for the twelve years she had spent with her husband and that she hoped to see him often in the future. "Joe is a wonderful bachelor and a wonderful stepfather," she wrote.[31] Even while publicly declaring the failure of her marriage, she hid her wounds under a veil of ironic affection.

So Susan Mary took her life into her own hands. She moved into an apartment rented to her by a friend, perched in the tall fortresslike complex called the Watergate. There had been a lot of talk about the Watergate since June 1972, when five men working for Richard Nixon's reelection committee were caught in the building trying to burglarize the Democratic Party headquarters. Their arrest had not harmed Nixon, who was reelected with relative ease. Over time, the president's role in the break-in leaked out. In May 1973, the Senate Watergate Committee hearings began. Susan Mary found them "horribly fascinating,"[32] but wanted to believe that the president had not known what was going on. However, it was revealed that a hidden system for recording conversations existed within the White House itself, and that the president was frantically doing all he could to hold up investigations.

The only good point of the apartment was its view of the Potomac, but Susan Mary always kept the curtains drawn because she thought the window frames too hideous. She also disliked the white walls, which she covered in paintings and the Watteau engravings of monkeys that she and Bill Patten had bought in Paris. The entryway was hidden behind a screen, and the chintz sofas and French furniture warmed up the three little rooms where Susan Mary received her guests. She told them calmly she was starting afresh, and said she missed nothing but her Georgetown garden. Her friends, who were not surprised by her separation from Joe, admired her nerve and almost believed in her high spirits.

It was not clear whether Susan Mary's unrelenting self-control hid deep suffering, or whether her delicate coolness kept her safe from the disorder of more violent emotions. Sometimes, in letters, the mask would fall and reveal something of her distress. "I am infinitely glad to be clearing out of here,"[33] she wrote to Marietta before joining her in Barbados in December. For once, the bougainvilleas, tropical punch, and relaxation beneath the white coral arches did nothing to restore her energy. "I feel like a piece of old wet flannel."[34] It took a stay in Florida on the plantation of her Whitehouse cousins and a few days at Marietta's house in New York to help her recover her strength and start reading again. Toward the end of January 1974, the psychoanalyst she had been talked into seeing found her in better form.

She had no regrets about leaving her husband, who was also shaken up by the separation, but she could not help addressing the subject in letters to her son, concluding, "Having loved him and fought for him was a waste of fourteen years."[35] This negative appraisal contrasted with the pathetically gushing tone of her letters to Joe himself. Before leaving for Barbados, she had thanked him for his Christmas present, a gouache by Hubert Robert, wishing that "despite the immense worry and sadness our marriage has given you, you will remember the happy times. There are so many."[36] Two months later, during which they saw and called each other regularly, she confessed her nostalgia: "Darling, I write to celebrate our wedding anniversary because it was such a good show—it lasted a long time and gave great pleasure to many people—above all to me. Looking at your high ceilings the other night, comparing them to my claustrophobic apartment, I felt how fortunate I had been, how much I owe to you, and how much I then and now loved you. Circumstances did not aid us, stars were crossed, but my marriage vows of February 16 hold."[37]

Holed up in an apartment she disliked, Susan Mary was confronted with painful loneliness. She still loved the man she had left, and felt burdened with the defeat of the separation for which she partially blamed herself. In spite of all this, she managed to begin a new life. She found strength in her friends and in the things that accompanied her in her Watergate exile, particularly an old typewriter and bundles of letters. The past had called out to her, welcoming, familiar, and infinitely malleable. She had decided to transform her life into a story. It was a metamorphosis that would be her salvation and greatest accomplishment.

IX

The Pleasure of Writing

From Paris with Love

The idea had come from Marietta. She and Susan Mary would gather their fifteen years of correspondence and offer it up to the public in celebration of their friendship. The book would have the added benefit of giving Susan Mary something to do and would add another jewel to Marietta's crown, proving she was as talented in literary matters as she was in politics and diplomacy. (Marietta had done a great deal for the Democratic Party before going on to represent the United States at the United Nations Commission on Human Rights under the Kennedy administration.) They went through old trunks and shoe boxes, and Marietta asked Ken McCormick, senior editor at Doubleday, to sample their letters. He read for fifteen minutes in the library of Marietta's New York town house while the two women smoked nervously in the room next door. Convinced by what he had seen, he told them to get started. A contract would arrive in the following day's mail.

The real work began early in the summer of 1973. Susan Mary

and Marietta had to unearth, sort out, and reassemble their correspondence. Both had kept almost everything they had written between 1945 and 1960, when Susan Mary was living in France and Marietta in England. Mrs. Jay also gave them the letters her daughter had sent her from Paris, which would be published as though they had been written to Marietta. As her friend had predicted, the discipline and pleasure of daily work calmed Susan Mary's frayed nerves and broken heart. Sitting at her felt-covered bridge table, she forgot the ugly apartment and let herself be carried back to her youth, that new and wonderful country one rushes through carelessly, vowing to return. With melancholy joy, she rediscovered the days of Bill's illness, the times when Duff used to take her on his lap, when gowns on loan from Dior waited in their tissue paper for her to make them bloom with triumphant flare. Without rewriting them entirely, Susan Mary shook out letters, removing old secrets and the most embarrassing cases of her naïveté as a wide-eyed American girl arriving on the Continent. She fretted over her banal style, frivolous preoccupations, and imprecise storytelling. Her editor, McCormick, regularly received anguished phone calls.

"I'll never make it. I'm going to throw it all in the Potomac."

"Do as you like. But I suggest you think twice and let me know how it's going next week."

Evening seemed to come all too quickly. With the help of her French maid, Mimi, she would clear off her worktable, light the candles, and prepare to greet her friends, the Bruces, Muffie and Henry Brandon, Carter Brown, Brooke Astor, Senator Heinz, and young Dallas Pell. She wanted her parties to be as exciting and successful as those she had hosted on Dumbarton Avenue. So she smiled encouragingly, listened intently, and had coffee served at the table to keep conversation going. The guests would leave around eleven, remarking on how well she was coping on her own. Her task completed, she could return to her beloved ghosts.

In 1974, almost all of Susan Mary's time was taken up by the book. Occasionally, she would pull away to listen to the rumors about Nixon's eagerly awaited resignation. Even Joe, who had always been careful never to weaken the president's position, had come to think that stepping down was the best thing Nixon could do. Still, Susan Mary was more interested in the events of the 1940s and 1950s than in current affairs. She read dozens of books on the period to make sure her notes and comments would be impeccable. Marietta had given up her share of the project, and the entire load now lay on Susan Mary's shoulders. In April, Doubleday sent her an advance of five thousand dollars, which she divided between her children. By November, the book was finished and Susan Mary decided to reward herself with a trip to Laos, where Charlie Whitehouse had been serving as American ambassador for a year and a half. She invited her sister-in-law Tish Alsop who had been a widow since Stewart Alsop's death in May, treating her to the journey. At the end of February 1975, the two women set off, intent on leaving their worries and solitude behind.

The ambassador's residence in Vientiane had a swimming pool and tennis courts, but Tish and Susan Mary had come to see something of the country. Charlie took them to meet General Vang Pao, the enemy of the Communist Pathet Lao and the CIA's faithful ally, who was based in Long Tieng, a mountain military fortress accessible only by air. The diminutive general was waiting, standing at attention in a khaki uniform decorated with three gold stars.

"Can't you just imagine him on horseback next to Genghis Khan?" Susan Mary whispered to her sister-in-law.

"Shush, he speaks English."

The general actually spoke a sort of soldier's French that was supplemented with expressive grimaces and gestures. He signaled to Charlie to sit next to him, while the ladies sat on a sofa with the first of the general's six wives. His officers stood behind him. They all drank warm whiskey that made Susan Mary's head spin. She watched lunch being prepared: large plates of white rice swarming with flies. As long as they serve it up quickly, she thought. Unfortunately, the general launched into a violent monologue, railing against the prime minister, Souvanna Phouma. "Ah, Ambassador, Souvanna is nothing but a woman, a frail little poplar tree all atremble even when there is no wind. You see, for us it's a life or death situation, and there's an 85% chance that we'll end up dead. Let's eat."[1]

The ordeal was not over. Like Levin in *Anna Karenina*, Vang Pao wanted to show his guests the agricultural progress that had been made among the local Hmong tribes under his command. The group boarded a beat-up helicopter with no doors or seat belts that the general piloted himself. The ancient machine lifted off with difficulty before sputtering high above the mountain valleys, where the mist rose like steam off a cup of tea. Susan Mary took refuge at the back of the cabin and shut her eyes, while Tish remained bravely seated at the edge of the precipice, working out whether her life insurance would cover her children's college education. Charlie mentally drafted their obituaries.

The next day's activities were less adventurous. Susan Mary and Tish toured Ban Houayxay, an outpost on the Mekong River. Martinis in hand, the two women sat watching the river. The sun was setting. A refreshing evening breeze carried the gentle sound of the nearby temple bells, and it was hard to believe that the Vietcong had passed through the sector only a day before. For the rest of the trip, when she was not flying around in a helicopter, Susan Mary was at the hairdresser's. There were a number of official dinners and lunches, and she wanted to honor the reputation of her cousin Charlie and not look windblown and unkempt among the silky Laotian princesses. She managed somehow, and Tish thought she looked as neat and elegant as usual, and far more relaxed. At the end of two marvelous weeks, they parted ways. Tish went back to the United States, and Susan Mary continued traveling, passing through Kuala Lumpur, Singapore, and Tehran, where her friends the Helms were posted. Finally, she stopped in London on her way to Washington. A month later, Saigon fell and the Pathet Lao seized power in Laos, driving out the royal court in Luang Prabang as well as the unfortunate Hmong who had trusted the United States.

On her return, Susan Mary resumed work on the book. Doubleday suggested a cover she described in a letter to Joe as "lovely and romantic, a collage which I think you will like. We owe (forgive me—I still say 'we') much to the blurbs which will be on the cover."[2] Arthur Schlesinger, Douglas Dillon, David Bruce, the actress Kitty Carlisle, and the popular author Emily

Kimbrough had all contributed their endorsements. These were printed with a photograph of Susan Mary in serious mode, her brow furrowed like a disapproving governess. "Those stern brown eyes," as Bill Patten used to say about his young wife. The book was dedicated to Mrs. Jay out of a sense of filial duty, but she was the most grateful to Joe and Marietta. Joe had supported her literary endeavors and allowed her to sign the book with the name Alsop, something her editor had insisted on. Marietta had not felt the slightest resentment after having chosen not to appear as a coauthor and was planning a reception in New York in September to celebrate publication. As to the book's actual content—"I am not ashamed,"[3] said Susan Mary when she received the first proofs. She even let herself show unusual self-satisfaction, repeating the compliments she had received ("David Bruce thinks my letters are better than Janet Flanner's"[4]) and comparing herself favorably to her old schoolmates, who "seem to have done so little with their potentialities. Rich, charming, everything going for them, now I flee when I meet one of them on the street."[5] Obviously, Marietta was not part of this depressing category, and Susan Mary continued to sing her praises. "You have done more with your life than any of our contemporaries. You are the star of our time."[6]

Of course, Susan Mary was capable of making things up out of pride, discretion, or the desire to spare her friends the chore of comforting her. This stoic politeness did not foster intimacy, but she had always preferred to serve herself a second glass of sherry rather than call out for help. Still, an optimistic tone, a little strained perhaps, began to color her mood in the spring of 1975. "Life ahead is going to be very gay."[7]

At last, it was time for rewards. The reviews in the *Washington Post*, the *New York Times*, and *Library Review* were all favorable. Readers also responded to the book, which went through six printings, selling more than twenty thousand copies. When *Letters to Marietta* was published in England the following year, Antonia Fraser praised it in an article titled "So Chic, So True, So Sad," noting the pertinent analyses and vivid style of a white-gloved reporter in postwar Paris who served up a mixture of politics and cosmopolitan life against the somber background of her husband's chronic illness.[8]

Like so many brownie points, Susan Mary collected her reviews and sent them to her family. She graciously accepted all requests for book signings and interviews. In fact, promoting the book was an unexpected pleasure. Finally, *she* was the person whom people were waiting for, listening to, and photographing.

For a November book tour in Texas, Oscar de la Renta suggested she wear a navy blue mohair coat over a dress in the same color. She arrived in Dallas on November 18 and was driven to bookstores in Doubleday's Cadillac. A chill went down her spine as she recognized the route, familiar to her from a fateful afternoon twelve years before. "I hear Jackie's voice in Dumbarton Avenue sitting on the sofa, clinging to Joe's hand: 'It was so hot, we turned the corner and I saw the underpass and thought, Oh, good, it will be cool for a few minutes, then I heard the shot, the first one.'"[9] Susan Mary also appeared on a popular television show and did so well that the channel's director offered to make her a reporter in Washington. Flattered, she refused, seeing a "mental picture of Joe's face if he hears that I am to do political reporting."[10] In her place, she suggested Sally Quinn or Barbara

Howar, both well-known journalists. She left Dallas for Austin,
where her friend Walt Rostow took her to a football game. It was
a real disappointment—there was not a single cowboy hat in the
entire stadium. The local men were dressed in tweeds, as though
attending a steeplechase in the south of England. So much for
local color. She gave a few radio and television interviews before
heading off to the university library to do research for her next
project.

The Adventures of Lady S.

The success of *Letters to Marietta* had encouraged Susan Mary to
begin work on a biography of a remarkable woman, Lady
Sackville. It was her English editor, George Weidenfeld, who had
suggested it.

Victoria Sackville had inherited her temperament and
impressive head of long black hair from her mother, a Spanish
dancer named Pepita. She spent her childhood in the difficult
position of an illegitimate child, for although Pepita was dearly
loved, she was not married to the English diplomat Lionel
Sackville-West, who had set up houses for his irregular family in
Paris and Arcachon. Upon Pepita's death in 1871, Victoria was
dispatched to a convent, then rescued and sent to Washington in
the capacity of hostess to her father, who had been appointed
plenipotentiary in the American capital. Queen Victoria and the
American First Lady approved of this rather daring initiative,
which suited eighteen-year-old Victoria very well. She knew she
was up to the task in spite of her total lack of experience.
Intelligent and willful, she did the job brilliantly, turning a

number of heads in the process. Her own remained steady. She wanted to marry money. When she returned to England with her father, who in the meantime had inherited Knole House in Kent and the title of Lord Sackville, she met her cousin, who also happened to be the handsome heir to her father's title and estate. Marriage followed. All her problems seemed solved; besides, she and her husband loved each other so much, it was said, that they never wanted to get out of bed in the morning. They soon had a daughter, Vita, who would become an author and the lover of Violet Trefusis and Virginia Woolf.

The marriage cooled after a few years, but Victoria was well on her way to fame, reigning over Knole House and her entourage of friends and dependents. She successfully fought two lawsuits filed against her, the first by one of her brothers who wanted his share of the family fortune, and the second by the family of John Murray Scott, who had inherited part of the Wallace Collection and had given some of it to his friend Victoria. Lady Sackville did not hesitate to defend herself in court and air out family secrets. She seduced the judges as easily as she had seduced the other men she crossed paths with, including J. P. Morgan, Lord Kitchener, Rudyard Kipling, William Waldorf Astor, Auguste Rodin, and especially the architect Edwin Lutyens, whom she tormented with an irresistible mixture of tenderness and aloofness. Her daughter and son-in-law, Harold Nicolson, were also treated to her violent whims and took them with less patience. Toward the end, there were so many family quarrels and reconciliations that Susan Mary—fascinated though she was by all that charm, fury, and bad faith—had trouble keeping everything straight.

Research on Lady Sackville began during the summer of 1975.

Kitty Giles, whom she had known since her time in Paris, got in touch with her cousin Nigel Nicolson and arranged a trip to England, during which Susan Mary stayed with Nigel at Sissinghurst and with Lord Sackville at Knole. Thanks to charming Kitty, Susan Mary was able to borrow suitcases full of family papers that she took with her to Maine, terrified at the idea that she might lose them at the airport. She spent months deciphering letters and other documents covered in Lady Sackville's tiny, faded, irregular hand, dictating them to her secretary, and blushing at the erotic descriptions of Victoria's honeymoon. She found a few more papers in Texas, but "nothing on Victoria, my girl. Naughty thoughts run through my mind—I sell everything I have here to the University of Texas under an assumed name, tell Nigel tearfully that documents have been stolen (having xeroxed them secretly), write Lady Sackville, retire to [the] finest villa in Tuscany, or should it be a château in Burgundy?"[11]

Susan Mary enlisted her friend Kay Evans to help her read old newspaper accounts of Washington diplomatic life. Every ten days, Kay would bring back a harvest from the Library of Congress, where she had been patiently combing through years of microfilmed newspapers.

When at last she started to write, Susan Mary found the task as difficult as research had been enjoyable. It was the first time she had actually tried to write a book, and her subject was a complex, multifaceted woman. In fact, one critic would later reproach her for not having captured the many nuances of Lady Sackville's character, unlike Nigel Nicolson, Victoria's grandson, whose book *Portrait of a Marriage* subtly depicts the loving but complicated relationship between his parents, Vita and Harold. This criticism seems unjustified, for although Susan Mary was interested in decor and described with evident relish the dresses and bibelots that ornamented her subject's life, she also managed to revive the turbulent emotions of a heroine more passionate than she herself was, but with whom she shared a taste for the French language, a love of art, diplomatic experience, and a certain *savoir-vivre*. Both Susan Mary and Lady Sackville knew how to behave. When they broke the rules, they did so with style.

To make things harder, Susan Mary was constantly interrupted because she could not and would not forgo her obligations to her family, friends, and Washington society. Joe, whom she often saw, invited her to a dinner for the Berlins with Henry Kissinger and to another for the Harrimans. She organized a reception in honor of Frank Wisner and his fiancée, Christine de Ganay. In August 1976, she went to Barbados to comfort the recently widowed Marietta, who felt lost and broken since Ronnie's death. After three exhausting weeks, she flew to Paris to attend her goddaughter Anne de Rougemont's wedding and visit Cy Sulzberger, who was mourning the loss of his wonderful wife, Marina, who had died in July. When Susan Mary finally came home, the presidential campaign was in full swing, pitting Gerald Ford against Jimmy Carter. It would be a political autumn.

"Is it true, Mrs. Carter, that when you and your husband find that you are filled with lust for someone of the other sex you kneel down one on each side of the bed and pray for guidance?"

"What nonsense, we have never done such a thing in our lives, who said that asinine thing?"

"Your husband, this morning, in Pittsburgh."[12]

If he was elected, Jimmy Carter had said he would do all he could to restore family values. This was not enough to convince Susan Mary to vote for him, and indeed, Gore Vidal was not alone in thinking that the Democratic candidate took his initials a little too seriously. On September 23, she gave a dinner party before the first of three televised presidential debates. All the journalists who were invited took notes. Joe was dismayed by the former Georgia governor's mediocre performance.

"He looked so tired, don't you think it was just that?" asked Susan Mary.

"Politicians are not permitted to get tired," Joe coldly remarked.[13]

In the end, Susan Mary decided to vote for Ford, "betraying my party and in hot disagreement with all my best friends."[14] Results had not been so close in sixty years. On election day, Joe took Susan Mary to New York. The vice president, Nelson Rockefeller, was having a party with a few friends in his enormous Fifth Avenue apartment to celebrate Henry Kissinger, who was about to leave the job of secretary of state, which he had held under the Nixon and Ford administrations.

"It is tragedy that his plans should be left unfinished,"[15] Joe lamented glumly, sitting next to Susan Mary in a bar later that evening. She was nearly as depressed as he was.

Joe never relented about President Carter, whom he criticized for his lack of realism and tendency to moralize. This was not true of Susan Mary, whose misgivings gradually evolved. Naturally, she also remained on friendly terms with Kissinger, who came one evening to watch one of David Frost's televised interviews with Richard Nixon. Feeling that the former president had minimized his role in foreign politics, Kissinger got himself into such a state that Susan Mary ended up writing a letter of protest to Nixon. He answered without delay: "I pointed out over and over that without Henry's creative ideas and diplomatic skills we would never have succeeded with our China initiative, the Soviet SALT I agreement, the Vietnam Peace Agreement and the progress toward reducing tensions in the Middle East. My own evaluation is that he will be remembered as the greatest diplomat of our times."[16] Susan Mary was asked to deliver the message to Kissinger.

While remaining faithful to old friends, Susan Mary made new ones as well. Always on the lookout for talent, she started inviting congressmen Tim Wirth and Bruce Caputo, noting, "I like the young men in this administration."[17] Figures from the past also reappeared, like Cyrus Vance, who, during a December dinner party in 1976, told the story of his recent nomination as Carter's secretary of state. Vance, who wanted the job, had spent a long day talking foreign policy with Carter in the president-elect's hometown of Plains, Georgia. At the end of the day, he still was not sure what his chances were.

"What time does your plane leave?" asked Carter.

"Seven thirty."

"Good. That will just give you time to help me cook dear little Amy's supper. Rosalynn is away."[18]

The two men cooked a hamburger, but dear little Amy was a picky eater and they had to put it back on the grill twice before she was willing to touch it. Then the dessert was not to her liking. Just as Vance started looking for his coat in desperation, Carter asked him if he would be so kind as to accept the job.

The most astonishing Washington saga from the Carter days was the meteoric rise of Pamela Harriman, "unquestionably the hostess of the new administration. It's sheer Trollope," wrote Susan Mary in a letter to a friend. "Kay Graham and Polly Fritchey are vitriolic about her, for they were the discoverers of Carter when Pam and Averell had dismissed him from their calculations; now Pam, the chameleon, has Brzezinski and the State Department Russia expert as permanent guests living in her house in swansdown comfort. She even dresses like Miss Lillian (Carter's mother) in simple jersey double knits. The Georgetown ladies rage."[19]

Susan Mary was fairly annoyed herself. She had never liked Pamela much since the old days when they were both in Paris. Pamela, who was divorced from Randolph Churchill, had once obliged the Pattens to put up her young son, Winston, while she and her lover, Giovanni Agnelli, holidayed in Italy. "When I think of my only friend who is a proper professional courtesan, and how pretty she looks, I feel pretty strongly that illicit love is the one that pays off,"[20] Susan Mary had written to Duff with the envious admiration she had never shaken off. She had been none too pleased to see Pamela move to Washington after her marriage to the old and wealthy Averell Harriman in 1971.

Still, such superficial irritation did not mar the overall satisfaction that Susan Mary felt during the autumn of 1977. She had finished her book and Nigel Nicolson had written to congratulate her. Her editors were delighted. She could finally take a much-needed break. More important, she had managed to achieve the two things she cared most about: keeping her place in society while living alone, and maintaining friendly, peaceful relations with Joe. One day, noticing that Susan Mary was feeling low, he sent her a comforting note. "Do not think of yourself as a 'tired, frail old lady.' You are an extremely beautiful woman, with a thousand friends and a great many people who love you, including me. We are both getting on a bit, but you don't show it, you give everyone a glorious time, and you have a long, rich life ahead of you."[21] Then Mrs. Jay died on Christmas Eve, typically causing, as Joe put it, "maximum inconvenience."

Two Houses of One's Own

No tears were shed at Susan Jay's funeral in Rye, New York. Surrounded by Joe, Bill, Anne and her husband George, and the tombs of the Jay ancestors, Susan Mary thought about her father and her own sad childhood. Of her mother, she would keep the memory of the invalid, paralyzed ninety-eight-year-old woman, a talkative and exacting snob to the last. Propped in bed, Mrs. Jay would tell people how she had attended the 1896 coronation of Czar Nicolas II wearing a green velvet dress that was later transformed into cushions—a model of the puritan economy that was typical of the Jay family, inspired not by poverty but by the rigid and virtuous rule that forbids waste.

Back in Washington, Susan Mary read the letters of condolence that had piled up on her desk, some five hundred pieces of evidence to the esteem that Mrs. Jay's dignity and advanced age had inspired in others. Replying was painful. "As only you and Bill have understood," she wrote to Joe, "I have been a distant, proper, efficient and rather unaffectionate daughter."[22] The only grief she felt was at feeling none.

Psychologically, Mrs. Jay's death was not a liberation; the damage caused by a lifetime of judgmental remarks was too deep. It was, however, a considerable and much-awaited material relief. Susan Mary now owned a substantial sum of money and two houses, one in the heart of shady Georgetown, the other, called Blueberry Ledge, in Northeast Harbor, Maine. Susan Mary had never really felt at home in Blueberry Ledge, but Mrs. Jay had always reminded her that it would be hers in a plaintive litany that eventually made her daughter long for it to come into her possession.

At the age of nearly sixty, Susan Mary was eager to be financially independent. To lighten her burden on Joe, they rapidly transformed their separation into a final divorce. She hoped her newfound freedom would allow her to live comfortably, be of financial assistance to her family, and keep both houses. Georgetown was the perfect setting for dinners and receptions and would guarantee her position on Washington's social chessboard. In Maine, her children and grandchildren would come to stay. These ambitions required careful investments. She took advice from Bill and her financial managers with the nervous anxiety of a child set loose in a candy store, money in hand, overwhelmed by the unaccustomed variety of choices and filled with the shy pride of having finally become a respectable customer.

The house in Georgetown at 1611 Twenty-ninth Street was in a sorry state. Large pieces of plaster fell sadly from the ceilings, and the walls were covered in an ancient, vague-colored damask that had never been very interesting. Susan Mary and her friend the New York decorator Nancy Pierrepont set to work. Upstairs, the bedroom and dressing room were redone in chaste simplicity. On the ground floor, they made the dining room cobalt blue to match the Sèvres china; the large sitting room just off the garden was done in green; and the library, where tea or cocktails were served, was decorated in dark red. Every time the new interior was photographed for *House and Garden*, the *Washington Post*, or the *Washington Star*, Susan Mary would say that many of the portraits were fakes and that if the house looked Victorian, it was due to the involuntary accumulation of objects over time, not to money or taste. This was pure coquetry, for no visitor could miss the quality of the Persian rugs, the Sargent portrait hanging above the mantelpiece, and the fine furniture, some of which had been left behind by Betty de Rothschild when she moved abroad to follow her husband. Even if deep armchairs did jostle with Parisian bergères, easy, unaffected comfort was not Susan Mary's way of doing things. Her new home had an elegance that was classically French—lean and stiff, with a gracious formalism livened up by strong colors, bow windows, and fresh curtains tied back like bouquets. The lamps had silk shades, and little porcelain containers filled with cigarettes sat on all the tables. The stage was set and ready for the actors.

"Many people have told us, Mrs. Alsop, that you're in great social demand in this city. What do you think?"

"Really? I wouldn't know. One never really knows when one is 'in.' Anyway, those lists, 'in,' 'out,' are often made up by journalists. Well, it's probably because I got to know a great many people through my former husband, Joe Alsop. I'm still on excellent terms with him. I think he's the best host in Washington."

"That may be because you still often serve as his hostess."

"What an odd idea. You are too kind. Take another cookie, my dear. No, thanks, not for me."[23]

In truth, Susan Mary knew exactly who she was and where she came from—genealogical concerns were one of the rare insecurities to which she was immune—and was also keenly aware of the quality of the circles she frequented in the United States and in Europe. Journalistic flattery of her social achievements in Washington did not impress her. In February 1988, *U.S. News & World Report* published a special issue on "The New American Establishment," in which seventy-year-old Susan Mary Alsop was placed among the fifteen most socially prominent people in the United States, in the company of Brooke Astor, Tina Brown, Malcolm Forbes, Ann Getty, Kay Graham, Norman Mailer, Jackie Onassis, Barbra Streisand, and Barbara Walters. Alphabetical arrangement put her at the top of the list. Pretending to be annoyed, she cut the article out, supposedly for her grandchildren.

What was her secret? Why did Henry Catto, the former chief of protocol to President Ford, the Kissingers, the Bradens, and the Brinkleys organize a book party for two hundred guests in honor of Susan Mary when *Lady Sackville* was published in October 1978? Why did so many foreign diplomats come to her house, such as Allan Gotlieb, Nicko Henderson, Michael Pakenham, and Hélie and Nadège de Noailles? Why was Nancy Reagan, who knew very few people when she arrived in Washington, keen to meet her? (Susan Mary gave a luncheon party for the First Lady in April 1981, shortly after the assassination attempt against the new president.) How was it that journalists like Jim Hoagland and John Newhouse, and political figures like Bob McNamara, Caspar Weinberger, and Brent Scowcroft, whom she thought the most intelligent among politicians,[24] never turned down an invitation from Susan Mary? It was at her house that Nigel Nicolson and Liliane de Rothschild came to stay. It was with her that young people arriving from Europe wanted to chat: Anne-Marie de Ganay, Bertrand du Vignaud, Nicole Salinger, and David Sulzberger, who was so funny, brilliant, and well informed. Sitting on the staircase, dressed in slacks and a cardigan, her hair parted on the side like a schoolgirl, Susan Mary would pull on the cigarette she held in her fingertips and say, "So, tell me what's going on in Paris these days."

Her charm and curiosity were still intact, as were the old-fashioned manners and the cut-glass diction that made her sound like a prewar movie star. She gave full, all-enveloping attention to her conversation partners—men in particular, but not exclusively—the kind of attention that made them sit up and feel more important, more alive. Subtly and firmly, she guided their performance. Those who did not want to deliver were not invited back, while those who were not capable of performing were not invited in the first place. She contributed to the show; history unfolded like a fan as she recounted stories about Roosevelt, Churchill, Ho Chi Minh, Greta Garbo in Chantilly, and Kennedy in the White House.

"What was I saying? Oh, yes, that weekend with the Windsors in Antibes. I was sick and they changed the sheets twice a day, which was rather tiring actually. Wallis forced me to come to the table for lunch even though I could barely sit upright. She wanted me to keep Paul Reynaud company because he didn't speak English very well. We finally broke with them because they thought General Marshall was a Communist. But you know, Charlie de Beistegui also asked me one evening whether Marshall came from a good family. Can you imagine? Oh, the French. That said, I don't want to get sentimental, I know them too well for that, but I'm just much happier in France than anywhere else. Oh, maybe I'll go back there one day."

She paused, a touch of sadness in her voice.

"Get yourself another drink and tell me about Star Wars again. I don't think I understood very well. What will become of the SALT agreements?"

There was something enchanting about Susan Mary. In the evening, the schoolgirl's look disappeared, and she shone, still very thin, wearing haute couture that had aged as well as she had. Dresses, stories, friendships, love affairs. She did not speak about her private life, but many knew about it. Philip Ziegler published a book about Diana Cooper in 1981 that mentioned the British ambassador's American mistress; however, Susan Mary and Diana's relationship remained unharmed. Then, in early 1986, John Charmley published a biography of Duff for which Susan Mary gave permission to quote her own letters, although she had long ago burned the ones she had received from Duff. The book got around, with even Karl Lagerfeld admiring the photograph of Susan Mary "taken at a Volpi ball in Venice, in which I look as if an elephant with big feet was taking a rest."[25] Hardly an elephant, this slim young woman in a white bustier, leaning toward her lover. After seeing Diana in London a few weeks before her death on June 18, 1986, she noted, "I am lucky to have had forty years of her friendship."[26]

By dint of her personality, exceptional talent as a hostess, and intelligent exploitation of her past, Susan Mary made her salon one of the centers of Washington social life, a place that evoked older, more civilized times, when money stayed in its place, political party affiliations were less important, and America got along with Europe. Becoming a legend has a price, and it was one that Susan Mary paid willingly. By inviting only those who were well known or hoped to be, by entertaining only success and ambition, she deprived herself of the other, gentler kinds of company that these strict criteria often cast aside. No matter her mood, she allowed herself only corseted perfection, sacrificing spontaneity, emotional sincerity, and repose. Even among her close friends, like Lorraine Cooper, Polly Fritchey, Vangie Bruce, and the highly amusing Oatsie Charles, she was rarely willing to take off the smiling mask she removed only in the presence of Marietta. One of her friends said that she was never sure which Susan Mary to expect, "one's old pal or the Duchess of Buccleuch." This remark would have probably pleased Susan Mary. Still, there was a different title she preferred to be called by, of which she felt increasingly worthy.

Tea with Edith Wharton and Other Stories

Lobster was so plentiful during the nineteenth century that servants in Maine often had contracts stipulating that they not be obliged to eat it more than twice a week. It had since become rarer fare, reserved for special times. The historian Olivier Bernier's 1979 visit was such an occasion. Susan Mary served the local delicacy before taking him to tea at Brooke Astor's. Back at the house, they sat on the white veranda perched above the rocks and blueberry bushes. The tips of the spruce trees caught the light of the setting sun. Bernier looked at the ocean. The view was spectacular and the house was simple, airy, and comfortably worn in all the right places.

"It's so lovely here in October," said his hostess. She was wearing the Maine summer uniform—pants, polo shirt, a silk scarf around her neck, and a straw hat. "The sun sets in the middle of the afternoon and one doesn't have to wait to have a martini. The sky's not even red yet, but we'll start now anyway. It will help us work."

Two glasses appeared.

"So, *cher* Olivier, you were telling me about what traffic was like in Paris in 1780."

"The carriages of the nobility clattered through at great speed, often causing loss of life and limb: there was actually a set tariff specifying the sum to be paid if you lost a leg, an arm, your life. Finally, the noise was so unbearable that straw was used to cover the street whenever people were ill. Of course, it soon decomposed and added to the mud."[27]

"How fascinating." Susan Mary was taking notes in a large black notebook. "Please, do go on."

The noise in the streets, Louis XVI's difficulty in consummating his marriage, competition among various Parisian salons: these were all details Susan Mary was gathering and weaving together into a new book, after having carefully verified their accuracy so the historians would not tear her to pieces.[28] To do so, she consulted experts and read through old manuscripts with the help of her assistant, Mary Buell. She also traveled to Madrid in search of traces of John Jay, and to Edinburgh to do research on Lord Stormont, ambassador to the king of England. She even climbed up to the attics of Versailles to find out how ladies wearing dresses over wide panniers managed on narrow staircases. In Paris, Jacques and Marie-Alice de Beaumarchais showed her the papers signed by John Jay in payment for the arms and ammunition shipment to the United States that their ancestor had organized and for which the American Congress later refused to pay, claiming the cargo was a gift from the French government.

Yankees at the Court was Susan Mary's third book. It told the story of the first American diplomats from the beginning of the Revolution to the end of Benjamin Franklin's service as an ambassador in 1785. The subject combined everything Susan Mary liked best: Paris, diplomacy, and the feats of her glorious ancestor. Doubleday published *Yankees at the Court* in the spring of 1982, and it appeared in a French translation the following year. Susan Mary had not tried to uncover anything new; rather, she wanted to present, in a lively fashion, the main events of a little known episode in Franco-American relations, which was, moreover, relatively static, for much of a diplomat's job is simply waiting as intelligently as possible. She explained the points still at issue among historians, and at times allowed herself to weigh in modestly and state her own position.

Susan Mary's prominence doubtlessly contributed to the book's success, and vice versa; this suited her perfectly. Before *Yankees at the Court* was even published, she had already begun work on a new book about the Congress of Vienna—*The Congress Dances*—this time for Harper & Row.

A few critics thought Susan Mary had been overambitious in choosing such a complex subject. No doubt, she simplified things, devoting more attention to the spectacle of Czar Alexander's arrival in Paris on March 31, 1814, the medieval tournament at the Hofburg, and the procession of royal sleighs at Schönbrunn than to the political consequences of the negotiations. She did not offer an opinion on whether the Congress of Vienna was responsible for a hundred years of European peace (as Henry Kissinger had maintained when she consulted him) or had merely preserved an archaic social order, which was blind and deaf to brewing national and social forces that would later take a terrible revenge. Still, she had no pretention of being more than an amateur, and she discussed the issue honorably enough while focusing on what interested her readers. Beside the male actors of the congress, she chose to follow the intrigues and affairs of three women: Dorothée de Talleyrand-Périgord, Wilhelmina de Sagan, and Princess Catherine Bagration. Susan Mary was far too proper to peek through history's keyholes and was always careful to protect the propriety of her heroines. Their bosoms remained covered, though at times the fabric was dangerously gauzy. Her book echoed with the sounds of waltzes and sabers clashing. Susan Mary was clearly amused by the boudoir diplomacy of the day, the elegant debauchery, the aristocratic bacchanals. She liked showing ambassadors and princes undone by the night's revelry and the difficulty of splitting up Saxony and heroic Poland. *The Congress Dances* tells of great events and of great lords and ladies, history of the kind that Susan Mary knew and understood. Duff strolls about in the book in the guise of Castlereagh or Talleyrand. "Mistresses here in Washington simply aren't as politically influential as they once were," she told the journalist Susan Watters. "I wish they were. It would be a lot more fun."[29]

The Congress Dances was published in the United States and Britain in the spring of 1984, and, like Susan Mary's previous works, it was well received. It would be her last book. Her poor eyesight, hardly improved by two cataract operations, forced her to give up research, much against her own will, for it had been an activity she had thoroughly enjoyed, both in itself and for its rewards. Her four books, together with a few literary reviews in the *Washington Post*, had lent to her reputation, put her on television, and brought her into lecture halls as Susan Mary Alsop, the writer. None of the women she knew, neither friends nor rivals, even the most beautiful, rich, and influential among them, could claim as much. She was proud to have her name printed in the card catalog of the Library of Congress, next to that of Joe, who, after retiring in 1974, had finished his magnum opus, *The Rare Art Traditions*, a universal history of art collecting, published in 1982. Susan Mary's achievements were, in effect, remarkable. In less than ten years, and no longer young, she had stirred up the energy and talent to build a literary career, all while maintaining one of Washington's most important political salons.

What was she to do with herself? She had never had much zeal for civic service or philanthropy, although out of friendship she gave some time to the foundation for abused children created by Evangeline Bruce in memory of her daughter Sasha, who had died tragically in November 1975. Stopping work altogether was inconceivable. She still felt she had not accomplished enough and wanted to continue earning money. For a while, she played with the idea of writing a mystery novel. Then Paige Rense, the dynamic editor of *Architectural Digest*, came up with a solution. Rense knew Susan Mary by reputation and was aware that she had an exceptional network of friends whose homes would be perfect subjects for *AD*. Would Mrs. Alsop be willing to accept a position as contributing editor? She would. Beginning in March 1984, her collaboration with *AD* lasted more than fifteen years, during which she wrote three to five articles a year, to the complete satisfaction of all involved.

Susan Mary had little trouble adjusting to *AD*'s stringent quality standards. Most of the time she had the ideas for her own articles, although she was occasionally sent on assignment. Each story required two photo shoots, the first a simple scouting mission and the second the definitive spread. Once the photographs were taken, she would do a tape-recorded interview. She had an excellent assistant, Jan Wentworth, who had worked for Walter Lippman and would soon enter Susan Mary's circle of close friends. Sometimes the interviews were conducted over the telephone, but Susan Mary also had the pleasure of going to Albi in 1986 to visit the former house of Toulouse-Lautrec and to Paris to see the rooms at the Travellers Club where Duff Cooper and Bill Patten had so often let loose and tippled, far from the prying eyes of women. Many doors opened: the Auchincloss family in New York, Teresa Heinz in Idaho, Lady Bird Johnson on her Texas ranch, Kay Graham in her Georgetown mansion, Ethel Kennedy in her office, former French first lady Claude Pompidou, and Canadian prime minister Pierre Trudeau. When she did an article on Blair House in Washington, where presidential guests stay, Reagan's chief of protocol, Selwa "Lucky" Roosevelt, thanked her in a kind note, calling her "a marvelous writer and a delicious friend."[30] From Riyadh to Moscow, Susan Mary's new job allowed her to discover new places and meet new people—it was interesting and respectable work, and it even paid well.

She wrote in the upstairs office of her Georgetown house after a light breakfast of an egg and a few pieces of toast, or an omelet at most. Faithful friends would come for tea in the afternoon.

These included Lucy Moorhead, Liz Stevens, her niece Teeny Zimmermann, and new additions Patsy Preston and Susan Brinkley. There were young men too—gifted young men always. She chatted about books with Roger Pasquier, and found Trevor Potter and John Irelan quite charming. There was also writer Leon Wieseltier, to whom she told the story of going to France in 1934 and meeting Edith Wharton. "A plump, elderly lady who seemed to me more upholstered than dressed with several scarves wound around a rather heavy, shapeless suit."[31] Far from home, Wharton was hungry for New York gossip, and young Susan Mary, who had hoped to hear illuminating talk of Proust and Bourget, soon grew bored. Now *she* was the one people doted on reverently. Oh, well. At least *she* had kept her figure. In Vidal-Quadras's portrait of her from 1985, she was still pretty and fetching, her shapely legs in fishnet stockings.[32] Her memories of visiting Wharton's home, Pavillon Colombe, served as the introduction to a collection of Wharton's short stories.

In the evening, Susan Mary continued to entertain or go out. When she and Joe were invited to the same party, she would pick him up in the little Honda that she drove dangerously fast. They talked on the telephone twice a day. Sometimes they would walk around Georgetown and look at familiar houses whose prices had become hair-raising. People would see them together, she in a hat, Joe stooping, leaning on a cane and touching the poles of the streetlights as he passed. "You are the wittiest and most diverting man alive," she wrote to him. "Washington would be a desert as far as I'm concerned if you weren't there."[33]

Susan Mary watched her grandchildren grow up with a pleasure that felt more natural than when Bill and Anne had been young. Anne's daughters, Katie and Molly Crile, sent her letters that she treasured, and on the Patten side of the family, she eagerly awaited visits from her grandson, Sam, who was already becoming interested in politics; from her granddaughter Eliza, who had her grandmother's eyes; and from the youngest, Sybil, to whom she wrote from Paris in September 1988, "I am so happy I may never leave Paris, except I want to see you."[34] Although they asked nothing of her, Susan Mary was always ready to pull strings and offer help. They told her about their studies and plans for life far more than their own parents had ever dared to do. At the time, always afraid to disappoint, Anne and Bill would gladly have traded their mother's high hopes for a few hugs. But Susan Mary, regrettably perhaps, had thought that ambition for her children was the best token of her affection.

In the summer, all three generations would get together at Blueberry Ledge in Maine. Joe, whom the children called Grandfather, often came along, as well as friends like David Sulzberger and Guido Goldman. Susan Mary would take the children to swim or play tennis, walking through the forest to Jordan Pond. In the evening, particularly when Marietta Tree was there, they would change for dinner. "Perhaps you'd like to go and brush your hair, Eliza?" Susan Mary would say casually, disguising her order as a useful suggestion. Although legally speaking she was no longer married to Joe, Anne had divorced and married John Milliken, and Bill and Kate had separated at the beginning of 1987, Susan Mary still referred to these times as family vacations, the sort of vacations she had never known as a child. When nobody was watching, she would pour herself another vodka and raise her glass in a silent toast.

X

And Night Came

Adieux

Susan Mary's affection for the irascible Joe was returned, and he never missed an opportunity to pay homage to the woman he no longer lived with. "We are closer to one another than most married couples I know," he wrote in the conclusion to his memoirs, adding, "And so the story, which still continues, has a happy ending."[1] Shortly after this declaration, their story came to an end. Joe had been suffering from lung cancer for two years when he died at home on August 28, 1989, watched over by his sister-in-law Tish and his faithful Italian caretaker, Gemma Pozza. Susan Mary was deeply affected, for they had been happy together as friends.

There was no question, however, of putting her sadness on display or slowing the rhythm of her activities. In the fall, she went to London to visit Henry Catto, who had just been appointed as American ambassador. Since Mrs. Catto was scheduled to visit the United States at the same time, a British newspaper published a photograph of Susan Mary with the headline AUNT SUE MARCHES IN AS HEIRESS FLIES OUT. In May 1990, Aunt Sue co-presided over a fund-raising event for the Sasha Bruce Foundation. The previous year, she had given the foundation some of her finest evening gowns for a charity auction, including a black sheath dress by Balmain that she had worn when Jackie Kennedy met General de Gaulle in the Élysée Palace on May 31, 1961. At Paige Rense's request, Susan Mary was put in charge of welcoming a group of interior decorators scheduled to give conferences at the Smithsonian Institution. They were thrilled to be invited to Mrs. Alsop's house and she enjoyed their company. "It is so odd to have sixteen people for dinner in Washington and nothing more serious than silk fringe mentioned. But it's a billion dollar industry and so its leaders are bright men and women."[2] Still, she remained more interested by current events, which included the "incredible"[3] happenings in Central and Eastern Europe in 1989, followed by the invasion of Kuwait and the Gulf War ordered by President Bush, a man she had not, until then, thought of as made of presidential stuff. She continued to be seen about town, refusing to admit that her strength might be starting to wane. At the beginning of 1991, during a holiday spent in Connecticut with her daughter's in-laws during which everybody, including her four granddaughters, caught the flu, she admitted to Cy Sulzberger, "I feel a hundred and fifty years old."[4] The year would soon bring another terrible blow.

At the age of only seventy-four, still active, admired, and full of life, Marietta Tree had been battling cancer for months. As she wanted to see the pine forests and the ocean one last time, she came to Blueberry Ledge at the end of June. Her extreme frailty made the short stay difficult. In the following weeks, Susan Mary called her in New York every day to hear the ever-worsening news, and spoke constantly of Marietta's condition to her friends Louise and Anne de Rougemont, who had come to stay in Maine during their summer holiday. On August 15, 1991, Marietta's battle ended. Grief stricken, Susan Mary managed to speak at the funeral service at Saint Thomas's in New York. "You are the complete companion of my life," she had written to her friend ten years earlier.[5] As long as Marietta was there, Susan Mary had been able to face life's hardships and to keep secrets. She had felt someone was holding her hand, giving her the safety she had known as a child until the Jays left Argentina, never again to celebrate Christmas as a family. Now, with her buttress gone, solitude would roam freely through her life.

The Confession

She kept up appearances. She continued to work for *Architectural Digest* and was constantly receiving visitors, as a revered yet accessible monument, "a cross between Alice Roosevelt Longworth and Betty Boop,"[6] one of her admirers used to say. An entire chapter in a little guide to Washington was dedicated to her, and she was featured in an article on Georgetown in *Town and Country* wearing a hat, an umbrella resting jauntily on her shoulder as if it were an accessory and not an ersatz cane.

When Maureen Dowd came for an interview, expecting to listen respectfully to a flow of memories, she found herself, to her surprise, caught up in an energetic discussion of Hillary Clinton's plans to reform health care.

"There's nothing sentimental about that woman. She's very impressive," declared Susan Mary admiringly.

"You've known everyone. Haven't you met the Clintons yet?"

"My dear girl, you're making me a glamour girl and I'm just an old lady."[7]

Her house remained a rallying point for English visitors to the American capital, such as writer Artemis Cooper, Duff's granddaughter, and her husband, historian Antony Beevor, or Princess Michael of Kent, for whom Susan Mary gave a dinner party to which Colin Powell was also invited. When she went to visit the diplomat Avis Bohlen in Paris, it was as though she were back in the old days, making the rounds of the couturiers and being feted by all her friends. People remarked on her elegance when she gave a black-tie party in June 1993 to celebrate the college graduation of her grandson, Sam. Three years later, Sam was stabbed trying to protect his grandmother from a mugger in the street. He emerged relatively unscathed from the event, and Susan Mary, who had kept her cool throughout, praised him for behaving like a Secret Service agent. Wearing a pomegranate silk dress with feathers in her hair and pearls in her ears, she was the belle of the ball organized by charming Pie Friendly for the centennial of the Washington Historical Society. While refusing the label, she kept up her reputation as "fashion doyenne" to the point of wearing gowns that were so fitted she could not remove them without assistance. One evening after dinner, Susan Mary pressed a friend to stay for a drink, then slipped away into the next room with the maid. There was a sound of rustling fabric, and Susan Mary returned, smiling, wearing a slightly different black dress.

"I revel in the thought of old age, think of all the time to read

Trevelyan and Toynbee and Balzac and hot water bottles and one's happy life to look back on," thirty-three-year-old Susan Mary had once told Duff.[8] What would she have said forty years later? Hot water bottles were, of course, available, but reading was increasingly difficult and memories were often painful. Scotch or vodka became necessary to make it through the day, waiting and waiting for the evening, which would hopefully bring company. Drink dissolved solitude, regrets faded into peaceful nostalgia, the end drifted further away.

The effects of this self-medication might have been less noticeable on a sturdier frame, but Susan Mary was extremely thin and hardly ate at all. Gemma, who had been looking after her since Joe's death, often had to call Bill or one of the grandchildren who happened to be at home to come and put a teetering Susan Mary to bed, the same Susan Mary with whom, earlier that afternoon, they had gone shopping or discussed the Maine Republicans' chances of keeping their seat in Congress. Distressing though it was, her family had to admit that sometimes their energetic, dignified, and exemplary grandmother had trouble remaining upright. There were multiple incidents during the summer of 1995—fainting and falls that often ended at the Mount Desert Island Hospital. Susan Mary would promise to try to control herself, but her children decided that goodwill alone was not enough and that they had to help their mother overcome her bad habits. There was a plan to move her to Utah to be closer to Anne, but it was not a good idea for her granddaughters to see her in such a condition. In short, something had to be done.

One October morning in 1995, Susan Mary was driven to a hotel room near Connecticut Avenue where her two children, her granddaughter Eliza, her assistant, Jan Wentworth, three of her closest friends—Polly Fritchey, Nancy Pierrepont, and Charlie Whitehouse—and a counselor from an alcohol treatment center were waiting. Each of them told her why she needed to get help—out of respect for those who loved her, and for herself. Poor Susan Mary thanked them all politely.

"There's a room reserved for you at Saint Mary's Hospital in Minnesota," the counselor gently explained.

"When do I have to go?"

"This afternoon."

"Oh, I'm afraid I'm not available this afternoon. I'm expecting people from *AD*." She flipped through her planner. "What about May?"

But she hated scenes and had to admit defeat. That same afternoon, Bill took the plane with his mother and accompanied her to Saint Mary's. Susan Mary saw the treatment as a trap from which she had to escape as soon as possible. For her family, it was a necessary step toward what they hoped might be a cure.

The treatment involved family therapy sessions. On October 31, 1995, during a meeting with Bill, Anne, John Milliken, and one of the hospital's counselors, Susan Mary began telling about Duff's death and Diana's courage in its aftermath. Bill did not understand the point of the story that the rest of the group seemed to be following expectantly. Then the therapist made a sign and Susan Mary, as though on cue, announced in an almost detached tone, "Oh, yes, of course, and he's your father."

Bill burst into tears and left the room.

In uttering that sentence, Susan Mary was obeying orders. Her daughter, who had known for a long time the identity of

Bill's real father, and the staff of Saint Mary's had insisted that she reveal what she had kept hidden for so long. Perhaps the confession was also her way of taking revenge for the treatment she was forced into, an undignified and quite useless ordeal, as she saw it. Perhaps she was unburdening herself. Or she may have thought that Bill, now forty-seven, was entitled to know the truth. It is hard to say whether she was speaking for her own sake, for her son's, or simply because she was made to. She never brought the matter up again and may have regretted speaking at all; but at the time, she must have felt an angry satisfaction at having caused chaos, a fitting epilogue to the unpleasant and embarrassing weeks she had undergone.

Shortly after the revelation, the burden of which was now Bill's alone, Susan Mary left the hospital.

The Summer of 2004

The stay at Saint Mary's was beneficial for a few years, then Susan Mary slowly returned to the comfort of alcohol, with all its inevitable consequences. The vain and tiresome struggle began anew between two children trying to protect their mother from herself and an aging woman who refused to accept the diagnosis and the treatment it entailed. She intended to continue living her life as always. Susan Mary was from a different generation born well before World War II that drank hard liquor like orange juice, inhaled smoke, and crossed the Atlantic on ocean liners. Gemma had returned to Italy, and sometimes the Philippine servants who had replaced her had their hands full. Panicked, they would call the hospital and Susan Mary would be whisked to the emergency room. "Let's get out of here," she once told Jan Wentworth, who had come to visit her.

Still, daily life was not all hardship. She wrote a few articles for *AD* and could still read with a magnifying glass. When she grew tired of this, she listened on tape to her favorite English authors: the Brontë sisters, Trollope, Dickens, Hardy, George Eliot, and Wilkie Collins. They were like the handrail on a rocky boat. During summers in Maine, she got together with her friends Nancy Pyne, Nancy Pierrepont, Bob and Sylvia Blake, Muffie Cabot, and Frankie FitzGerald. She walked more slowly, but she still went on the same strolls, stopping when she was overwhelmed by vertigo. In 2000, she managed to visit her niece Maisie Houghton, who lived on an island south of Northeast Harbor. In 2001, she received Béatrice de Durfort, Louise de Rougemont's granddaughter. Dinners continued, Susan Mary bravely keeping a busy social calendar at the age of eighty. People continued to meet in her house, like columnists Kevin Chaffee and Dominick Dunne (the latter recounted the details of the Monica Lewinsky scandal, which Susan Mary thought utterly silly). When Amanda Downes from the British Embassy or the French curator Sylvain Bellenger came to tea, they found a woman whose hair and makeup were done and who still knew all the latest political gossip. She impressed biographer Sally Bedell Smith with her precise memories of the Kennedys; journalist Sally Quinn was struck by how well informed she was. Each of these encounters was a carefully prepared performance, usually pulled off with success. Keeping the flag flying was a duty, one that helped Susan Mary keep away sadness and loneliness.

Apart from her granddaughters' visits (Sam was working

abroad at the time), one of Susan Mary's greatest joys during those years was her friendship with Rob Brown and Todd Davis, two interior decorators who, in the spring of 1996, had bought and renovated the house next door. Wary of the welcome that they would receive in a neighborhood that had a reputation for disliking noise and novelty, they presented themselves at Mrs. Alsop's door with orchids. Someone in a pink dressing gown appeared behind the maid. Susan Mary exclaimed at the beauty of the flowers and invited them to sit on the stoop. They started chatting.

"I'm having a little dinner party for some friends and I'd be so pleased if you could come. But perhaps you'd find it dull."

Todd and Rob politely accepted the invitation, expecting an old ladies' party. On the said evening, they found themselves in an immaculate dining room with an experienced hostess who introduced them to Paige Rense and the British ambassador's wife. Decorating jobs soon came their way and their careers were officially launched, as Susan Mary had hoped. The trio became inseparable. The young men invited Susan Mary to their house or took her to Galileo, a fashionable Italian restaurant. She showed them Maine as she knew it, blithely ignoring the NO TRESPASSING signs—after all, Mount Desert Island was her home—taking them to David Rockefeller's gardens and Martha Stewart's house where she had danced as a girl.

In 2001, her "dear boys" left Washington. That same year, Charlie Whitehouse died, followed by Kay Graham. Evangeline Bruce had passed away in 1995. "We're all so old or dead. There's almost no one left."[9] Susan Mary was still there, but she was finally starting to look her age.

Her condition began to worsen during the summer of 2002. Her lungs functioned poorly and fatigue could not be resisted. She went to Maine one last time, and, in September, attended the marriage of her beloved granddaughter Eliza. Back in Washington, she stopped the parties and the writing for *Architectural Digest*. Everything was becoming difficult and she took to her bed. Lying there, she listened to Jim Lehrer's *NewsHour* at six every evening. Family and friends, Kay Evans, Pie Friendly, her Zimmermann nephews, Deedy Ogden, and Jan Wentworth, surrounded her with devoted care. Anne came regularly from Utah and took care of everything. People found Susan Mary calm; at times she had a vacant look about her, though when her alertness returned, she always had a kind word for them. They took turns reading to her, especially Bill Blair, her childhood friend from Bar Harbor, the first boy with whom she had gone to the movies. Now a retired ambassador, he came to see her three times a week at two in the afternoon. He would go upstairs and read to her from the *New York Times*, biographies, and Cecil Beaton's memoirs, avoiding passages that mentioned Duff. Sometimes the phone would ring and Bill Blair would see her pick it up with sudden energy. Susan Mary was not in pain but she slept a lot. It was as though she were watching her own exit from the world; since the show did not please her, she preferred to keep her eyes shut.

At the beginning of 2004, it became clear that life was leaving her tired little body. In early summer, her family gathered around her for a farewell. Afterward, Susan Mary, who had always avoided emotional display, merely asked if there was any cake left. Bill went to France to join his wife, Sydney, in the Pyrenees, where they had a house in the high Luchon valley. Anne stayed on with Susan Mary for a few peaceful and loving weeks. She had always known how to make her mother smile, and their final days together were sweet. On the afternoon of August 18, she called her brother to tell him that it was all over. Bill went out into the garden. Night had fallen and the stars lit up the sky over France.

It rained when Susan Mary's ashes were scattered over the ocean off the coast of Maine, but the weather was beautiful on September 24, 2004, the day of the funeral service at Christ Church in Georgetown, the church Susan Mary had attended every Sunday. She would have been glad to hear the words that were spoken in her memory, to see the grace and dignity with which her granddaughters took care of those in attendance, and the number of people who filled the church. She would have also liked the articles that appeared in American and British newspapers in homage to her extraordinary life. The chorus of praise called her a legendary hostess, an American aristocrat, and the witness of a bygone era. Some pointed out that this true lady had been known by her given name, a tender and mischievous name, almost childish—Susan Mary. It was what everybody called her.

Acknowledgments

As stated at the beginning of the Sources and Bibliography, most of the sources on Susan Mary Alsop come from her family's personal archives, kindly put at my disposal by Susan Mary's son, William S. Patten. I would like to express my profound gratitude for the trust and generosity Mr. Patten has shown since our first meeting in the summer of 2006 in his beautiful house in the French Pyrenees where he and his wife, Sydney, regularly stay. Bill and Sydney were also kind enough to welcome my sister, Aniela Vilgrain, who helped with this project, to their former home in Massachusetts. The project then began to shuttle back and forth between Aniela's house in Washington, where she lives, and my home in France. All these meetings gave birth to a friendship that is very dear to both Aniela and me.

I would also like to thank Anne Milliken, Susan Mary's daughter, for her valuable assistance and the warm hospitality she and her husband, John, extended to Aniela, whom they invited to Salt Lake City, where Anne spoke with Aniela at length about her mother. I also had the pleasure of meeting Susan Mary's grandchildren Sam and Sybil Patten, and having a telephone conversation with Eliza Patten.

David Sulzberger was immediately interested in the project and he proved endlessly helpful, efficient, and generous in Paris, London, and New York. His part in this book is an important one, and I am most grateful to him.

I will never forget the London spring of 2009, during which I worked in Lord Norwich's library and in the house of his daughter, my friend Artemis Cooper. It was thanks to them, and through the letters they allowed me to read, that I got to know Susan Mary as a young woman in love. I hope that John Julius and Molly Norwich and Artemis and Antony Beevor find in these words the expression of my profound gratitude. I would also like to thank Lord and Lady Thomas, who helped me to understand an important time in Susan Mary's life.

My friends also took part in this project. Sybil d'Origny went with me to Newport, Rhode Island, and introduced me to many of her American cousins and friends; Charlotte Mosley put her library at my disposal. I owe them both a great deal. It is also a pleasure to thank François Stasse, Denis Bourgeois, Thierry Tuot, Pierre Morel, and Hélène Vestur for their advice and support.

It was important for me to know the places where Susan Mary once lived. Thanks to Irene Danilovich, I was able to visit the house in Georgetown where Susan Mary lived during her marriage to Joe Alsop. Aniela visited the house in Northeast Harbor during a stay in Maine with Malcolm and Pamela Peabody; the late Mr. and Mrs. David Ridgely Carter showed me their lovely house in Senlis. Thanks to Lady Westmacott, wife of Sir Peter Westmacott, former British ambassador to France and present ambassador to the United States, and to the erudite Ben Newick, I was able to see the British ambassador's residence in Paris as I had never seen it before. I am very grateful to both of them.

Aniela and I would also like to thank the following friends, family, and relations of Susan Mary Alsop for having spoken with us or provided us with source material:

In the United States: Patricia Alsop, Katharine Jay Bacon, Olivier Bernier, William McCormick Blair Jr. and Deeda Blair, Sylvia Blake, Avis Bohlen, Benjamin Bradlee, Rob Brown, Thomas and Constance Bruce, William Buell, Mabel Brandon Cabot, Marion Oates Charles, Todd Davis, Amanda Downes, Frederick Eberstadt, Kay Evans, Frances FitzGerald, Alfred and Pie Friendly, Guido Goldman, Cynthia Helms, Jane Stanton Hitchcock, James Hoagland, Nancy Hoppin, Maisie Houghton, John Peters Irelan, Yves-André Istel, Rhoda Kraft, Walter Lippincott, James G. Lowenstein, Lucy Moorhead, Timothy Mortimer, John Newhouse, Paige Rense Nolan, Deedy Ogden, Roger Pasquier, Dallas Pell, Nuala Pell, Ann Pincus, Trevor Potter, Dr. Christina Puchalski, Nancy Pyne, Sally Quinn, Rudolph Rauch, Susan Rauch, Alexandra Schlesinger, Caroline Seebohm, Sally Bedell Smith, Elizabeth Stevens, James Wadsworth Symington, Mario d'Urso, Jan Wentworth, Janet Whitehouse, Sheldon Whitehouse, Leon Wieseltier, Elizabeth Winthrop, Frank G. Wisner II and Christine Wisner, and Corinne Zimmermann.

In Great Britain: Lady Berlin, Lady Camrose, the Dowager Duchess of Devonshire, Sir Frank and the late Lady Katherine Giles, Mrs. H. J. Heinz, the late Sir Nicholas Henderson, Sir Michael Pakenham, and Lord Weidenfeld.

In France: Ambassador Benoît d'Aboville, Mrs. Jacques Andréani, Mrs. Jacques de Beaumarchais, Jean-Pierre de Beaumarchais, Sylvain Bellenger, Georges Berthoin, Celestine Bohlen, Bobby Bordeaux-Groult, the late Comtesse Diane de Castellane, Charles de Croisset, Béatrice de Durfort, Anne-Marie de Ganay, the Marquise de Ganay, Pierre Hassner, the Duc de Lorge, Jean-Claude Meyer, Bernard Minoret, the late Duc de Mouchy, Nelly Munthe, Ivan Nabokov, Victoria de Navacelle, Yvan de Navacelle, the Duc and Duchesse de Noailles, William Pfaff, Anne de Rougemont, Nicole Salinger, and Bertrand du Vignaud.

In Italy: Gemma Pozza.

My sister and I would also like to thank all those who offered us advice or lent us books during our research: Marie-Françoise Audouard, Charles Bremner, Malcolm Byrne, Irène Chardon, Florence Coupry, James Davison, Janice Frey, Peter Halban, Professor Gregg Herken, Basil Katz, Marc Lambron, Sarah de Lencquesaing, Charles McGettigan, Michael Mallon, the late Helen Marx, Claire de Montesquiou, Beverly Montgomery, Candice Nancel, Elena Prentice, Elaine Sciolino, Alex Tancredi, Charles Trueheart, Hubert Védrine, and, of course, Stanislas, Jean-Rodolphe, Donatella, and Alexandra Vilgrain.

My mother was an eagle-eyed reader and translated Argentine newspaper articles for me. I would like to thank her warmly as well as my mother-in-law, who shared her Washington memories of Susan Mary with Aniela and with me.

Thank you, Gilles, for listening to me tell a story evening after evening for an entire year, a story that he now knows as well as I do.

I am also very grateful to Mr. Jean-Marc Sauvé, the vice president of the French Conseil d'État, and to presidents Bernard

Stirn, Pierre-François Racine, and Edmond Honorat, as well as to Mr. Christophe Devys for making it possible to bring this project to fruition.

This book would not have been done without my sister, Aniela. Her understanding of the United States and her intimate knowledge of Susan Mary were essential to me. I thank her from the bottom of my heart.

Finally, I would like to thank my editors at Robert Laffont, Malcy Ozannat and Dorothée Cunéo, who gave me the idea to write this book in the first place; Benita Edzard and Gregory Messina, who launched it on its transatlantic journey; Kathryn Court, who decided to publish it; Christopher Murray, who translated it; and Tara Singh, who watched over it at Viking.

Notes

III. PARIS

1. Susan Mary Alsop, *To Marietta from Paris, 1945–1960* (New York: Doubleday, 1975), 9. (Hereafter, *Marietta*.)
2. Adapted from *Marietta*, 23.
3. *Marietta*, 31.
4. *Marietta*, 61.
5. *Marietta*, 33.
6. Adapted from *Marietta*, 34–35.

IV. AFFAIRS OF THE HEART

1. Jean Cocteau, *Journal, 1942–1945*, ed. Jean Touzot (Paris: Gallimard, 1989), 597.
2. As cited in Diana Cooper, *Autobiography* (Salisbury, United Kingdom: Michael Russel, 1979), 730.
3. *Marietta*, 64.
4. *Marietta*, 83.
5. Duff Cooper, *The Duff Cooper Diaries*, ed. and introduced by John Julius Norwich (London: Phoenix, 2006), 436.
6. Letter from Susan Mary to Duff Cooper, April 23, 1947. All letters from Susan Mary to Duff Cooper come from the Cooper family archives. All other letters come from the Patten family archives, except when noted otherwise.
7. Letter from Susan Mary to Duff Cooper, April 29, 1947.
8. Ibid.

9. Cooper, *Duff Cooper Diaries,* 417. *Copain* (pal) is in French in the original.
10. Cocteau, *Journal, 1942–1945,* 620.
11. Letter from Susan Mary to Duff Cooper, May 20, 1947.
12. Cooper, *Duff Cooper Diaries,* 438.
13. Duff Cooper's unpublished diary, July 6, 1947.
14. Letter from Susan Mary to Duff Cooper, September 24, 1947.
15. Letter from Susan Mary to Duff Cooper, June 30, 1947.
16. The quote means "Tonight I love you too much to talk to you of love." (This quote is from a poem by Paul Géraldy.)
17. Letter from Susan Mary to Duff Cooper, July 4, 1947.
18. Letter from Susan Mary to Duff Cooper, May 15, 1947.
19. Cooper, *Duff Cooper Diaries,* 449–50.
20. Letter from Susan Mary to Duff Cooper, October 8, 1947.
21. Duff Cooper's unpublished diary, October 15, 1947.
22. Letter from Susan Mary to Duff Cooper, May 26, 1947. *Frondeurs* are "troublemakers."

V. THE AGE OF SERENITY

1. Duff Cooper's unpublished diary.
2. Cooper, *Duff Cooper Diaries,* 460.
3. Nancy Mitford, *The Letters of Nancy Mitford and Evelyn Waugh,* ed. Charlotte Mosley (London: Hodder & Stoughton, 1996), 92.
4. Letter from Susan Mary to Duff Cooper, July 5, 1948. Georges Bidault and Jules Moch were the minister of foreign affairs and the minister of the interior, respectively, in Robert Schuman's cabinet from November 1947 to July 1948.
5. Duff Cooper's unpublished diary, July 7, 1948.
6. Duff Cooper's unpublished diary, July 13, 1948.
7. Letter from Susan Mary to Duff Cooper, October 26, 1948.
8. Letter from Susan Mary to Duff Cooper, August 15, 1948.
9. Nancy Mitford, *Letters of Nancy Mitford and Evelyn Waugh,* 114–15.
10. Letter from Susan Mary to Duff Cooper, August 25, 1948.
11. *Marietta,* 140.
12. Letter from Susan Mary to Duff Cooper, March 2, 1949.
13. *Marietta,* 136.
14. Letter from Bill Patten to Susan Mary, March 4, 1949.
15. Nancy Mitford, *The Blessing,* in *The Nancy Mitford Omnibus* (London: Penguin, 2001), 388.
16. Letter from Susan Mary to Duff Cooper, March 3, 1949.
17. Duff Cooper's unpublished diary, March 2, 1950.

18. Letter from Susan Mary to Duff Cooper, March 3, 1950.
19. Duff Cooper, *Duff Cooper Diaries,* 473.
20. Letter from Susan Mary to Duff Cooper, March 9, 1949.
21. Letter from Susan Mary to Duff Cooper, March 20, 1950.
22. Lord Granville, an English diplomat, had a long affair, mostly but not exclusively epistolary, with Lady Bessborough at the beginning of the nineteenth century.
23. Selina Hastings, *Nancy Mitford* (London: Papermac, 1986), 161.
24. Mitford, *The Blessing,* 388.
25. Nancy Mitford, *Don't Tell Alfred, in The Nancy Mitford Omnibus,* 517.
26. Mitford, *Don't Tell Alfred,* 519.
27. Mitford, *Don't Tell Alfred,* 520.
28. Mitford, *Don't Tell Alfred,* 575.
29. Mitford, *Don't Tell Alfred,* 576.
30. Letter from Susan Mary to Duff Cooper, July 11, 1947.
31. Letter from Susan Mary to Gladwyn Jebb, August 24, 1960.
32. *Marietta,* 176.
33. Letter from Susan Mary to Duff Cooper, April 10, 1951.
34. Letter from Susan Mary to Duff Cooper, July 16, 1950.
35. Letter from Susan Mary to Duff Cooper, July 11, 1950.
36. Letter from Susan Mary to Louise de Rougemont, August 30, 1950, Rougemont family archives. (In French in the original.)
37. *Marietta,* 179.
38. *Marietta,* 183.
39. Paul Morand, *Venises* (Paris: Gallimard, 1971), 160.
40. Jean Cocteau, *Le Passé défini,* vol. I, *1951–1952* (Paris: Gallimard, 1983), 35.
41. Edmond was her butler.
42. Letter from Susan Mary to Duff Cooper, December 26, 1951.

VI. WHEN SHADOWS FALL

1. Letter from Susan Mary to Duff Cooper, July 8, 1953. (In French in the original.)
2. Letter from Susan Mary to Duff Cooper, August 10, 1952.
3. Letter from Susan Mary to Duff Cooper, November 25, 1950.
4. Letter from Susan Mary to Duff Cooper, July 2, 1950.
5. Letter from Susan Mary to Duff Cooper, September 8, 1952.
6. Nancy Mitford, *Love from Nancy: The Letters of Nancy Mitford,* ed. Charlotte Mosley (London: Hodder & Stoughton, 1993), 359.
7. Cited in Janet Flanner, *Paris Journal, 1944–1955* (San Diego, Calif.: Harvest Books, 1988), 118.

8. Supreme Headquarters Allied Powers Europe.
9. *Marietta*, 232.
10. *Marietta*, 246.
11. *Marietta*, 247.
12. *Marietta*, 178.
13. *Marietta*, 283.
14. Letter from Nancy Mitford to her sister Jessica in *The Mitfords, Letters Between Six Sisters,* ed. Charlotte Mosley (New York: HarperCollins, 2007), 291.
15. *Marietta*, 296.
16. Adapted from *Marietta*, 327.
17. Letter from Bill Patten to Susan Mary, June 30, 1959.
18. Letter from Bill Patten to Susan Mary, July 5, 1959.
19. Letter from Susan Mary to Gladwyn Jebb, August 24, 1959.
20. Letter from Susan Mary to Gladwyn Jebb, August 15, 1959.
21. Letter from Susan Mary to Gladwyn Jebb, August 7, 1959.
22. Letter from Susan Mary to Gladwyn Jebb, August 3, 1959.
23. Letter from Susan Mary to Gladwyn Jebb, August 24, 1959.
24. Ibid.
25. Ibid.
26. *Marietta*, 348.
27. Letter from Susan Mary to Gladwyn Jebb, April 6, 1960.
28. Cited in a letter from Susan Mary to Gladwyn Jebb, March 30, 1960.
29. Letter from Nancy Mitford to Susan Mary, October 30, 1960.
30. Letter from Susan Mary to Gladwyn Jebb, June 28, 1960.

VII. AT THE COURT OF KING JACK

1. "I'm back from the States—full of stories about the court of King Jack at Washington." Letter from Diana Cooper to Evelyn Waugh, March 15, 1963, in *Mr. Wu and Mrs. Stitch: The Letters of Evelyn Waugh and Diana Cooper,* ed. Artemis Cooper (London: Sceptre, 1992), 398.
2. Cited in a letter from Susan Mary to Gladwyn Jebb, August 14, 1960.
3. Ibid.
4. There are several versions of the Moscow incident of February 1957. I have based my account on the CIA file, which includes letters from CIA director Allen W. Dulles to FBI director J. Edgar Hoover dated March 27 and April 1, 5, and 16, 1957. The letter from April 1, 1957, contains a memorandum written by Joe Alsop in Moscow. For the incident's consequences, I have followed Robert W. Merry's biography of Joe and Stewart Alsop,

Taking on the World: Joseph and Stewart Alsop, Guardians of the American Century (New York: Penguin, 1997), 363, 591–92.

5. Letter from Susan Mary to Marietta Tree, December 2, 1960.

6. Letter from Susan Mary to her mother, January 4, 1961.

7. Letter from Frankie FitzGerald to Susan Mary, January 16, 1961.

8. William S. Patten, *My Three Fathers and the Elegant Deceptions of My Mother, Susan Mary Alsop* (New York: Public Affairs, 2008), 191.

9. Letter from Susan Mary to Joe Alsop, November 3, 1976, from the Joseph Alsop and Stewart Alsop Papers, Library of Congress, box 224. (Hereafter, JA and SA Papers.)

10. Adapted from a letter from Susan Mary to her mother, January 25, 1961.

11. Several books on the Kennedys, seldom the best ones, hint or even state that the newly elected president took to bed one or even several of the women present that evening at Joe Alsop's house. For a discussion and refutation of this claim, see Patten, *My Three Fathers,* 205–6, and Merry, *Taking on the World,* 358, 591.

12. Cited in Sally Bedell Smith, *Grace and Power: The Private World of the Kennedy White House* (New York: Random House, 2004), 378.

13. The date of this dinner varies according to the source. Susan Mary mentions it without specifying the date in *Marietta* (42–43), as does Joe Alsop in his memoirs, *"I've Seen the Best of It"* (446–48). Charles E. Bohlen gives the date as October 18, 1962, in his book *Witness to History* (489). Robert Merry in *Taking on the World* (384) and Walter Isaacson in *The Wise Men* (623, note 802) say October 17. Richard Reeves in *President Kennedy: Profile of Power* (377), Arthur Schlesinger in *A Thousand Days* (802), Sally Bedell Smith in *Grace and Power* (312), and Katharine Graham in *Personal History* (295–96) all date the dinner to October 16. I have chosen to side with the latter date because it corresponds with the copy of the White House agenda of President Kennedy accessible on the Web site of the John Fitzgerald Kennedy Library. This is also the date mentioned in Sir Isaiah Berlin's interview with Arthur M. Schlesinger Jr. recorded on April 12, 1965, for the John Fitzgerald Kennedy Library Oral History Project.

14. Adapted from a letter from Susan Mary to Marietta Tree, June 26, 1963.

15. Letter from Susan Mary to Avis Bohlen, December 2, 1963, from the Marietta Tree Papers in Harvard University's Arthur and Elizabeth Schlesinger Library on the History of Women in America, Radcliffe Institute for Advanced Study. (Hereafter, Radcliffe.)

16. Joseph W. Alsop, interview recorded by Elspeth Rostow, June 26, 1964, John Fitzgerald Kennedy Library Oral History Project, 99.

17. Letter from Susan Mary to Avis Bohlen, December 2, 1963.

18. Letter from Susan Mary to Joe Alsop, November 3, 1976, JA and SA Papers, box 224.

19. Undated letter from Susan Mary to Marietta Tree, probably autumn 1964.

20. Letter from Susan Mary to Joe Alsop, November 3, 1976.

21. Letter from Susan Mary to Marietta Tree, July 1, 1967.

VIII. ANATOMY OF A MARRIAGE

1. Letter from Susan Mary to Avis Bohlen, October 1968, Radcliffe. *Cela vaut la peine* means "It's worth it."

2. Adapted from a letter from Susan Mary to her son, December 2, 1964.

3. Letter from Susan Mary to her daughter, March 11, 1969.

4. Letter from Susan Mary to Joe Alsop, August 30 (year not indicated), JA and SA Papers, box 128.

5. Letter from Susan Mary to Joe Alsop, July 28, 1969, JA and SA Papers, box 128. *Va-et-vient* means "coming and going."

6. Letter from Susan Mary to Joe Alsop, September 22 (year not indicated, probably 1966), JA and SA Papers, box 128.

7. Ibid.

8. Letter from Susan Mary to Joe Alsop, July 5, 1969, JA and SA Papers, box 128.

9. Letter from Susan Mary to Joe Alsop, July 22, 1969, JA and SA Papers, box 128.

10. Letter from Susan Mary to her son, March 15, 1970.

11. Ibid.

12. Ibid.

13. Ibid.

14. Letter from Richard Nixon to Susan Mary, May 8, 1970, JA and SA Papers, box 134.

15. Letter from Susan Mary to Joe Alsop, November 3, 1976, JA and SA Papers, box 224.

16. Art Buchwald, *Sheep on the Runway* (New York: G. P. Putnam's Sons, 1969), 133–35.

17. Letter from Susan Mary to Joe Alsop, November 22, 1970, JA and SA Papers, box 128.

18. Letter from Joe Alsop to Mrs. Adams, November 2, 1970, JA and SA Papers.

19. Letter from Susan Mary to her son, August 2, 1968.

20. Letter from Susan Mary to Marietta Tree, July 29, 1968.

21. Letter from Susan Mary to her son, October 1969.

22. Letter from Susan Mary to her son, January 11, 1972.

23. Undated letter from Susan Mary to her son, probably from the spring of 1972.
24. Adapted from a letter from Susan Mary to her son, February 12, 1971.
25. Notes taken by Susan Mary during a dinner at the White House on March 29, 1972, recounted in a letter to her son, March 31, 1972.
26. Letter from Susan Mary to Marietta Tree, November 22, 1972.
27. Cited in Merry, *Taking on the World*, 508.
28. Letter from Susan Mary to Joe Alsop, November 3, 1976.
29. Marina Sulzberger, *Letters and Diaries of Marina Sulzberger*, ed. C. L. Sulzberger (New York: Crown, 1978), 458.
30. Letter from Susan Mary to Joe Alsop, July 28, 1969, JA and SA Papers, box 128.
31. Merry, *Taking on the World*, 519.
32. Letter from Susan Mary to her son, May 17, 1973.
33. Letter from Susan Mary to Marietta Tree, November 29, 1973, Radcliffe.
34. Letter from Susan Mary to her son, January 7, 1974.
35. Letter from Susan Mary to her son, cited in Patten, *My Three Fathers*, 267.
36. Letter from Susan Mary to Joe Alsop, December 16, 1973, JA and SA Papers, box 128.
37. Letter from Susan Mary to Joe Alsop, February 23, 1974, JA and SA Papers, box 128.

IX. THE PLEASURE OF WRITING

1. Letter from Susan Mary to Mary Whitehouse, March 3, 1975, Whitehouse archives. The quote is in French in the original letter.
2. Letter from Susan Mary to Joe Alsop, May 1, 1975, JA and SA Papers, box 224.
3. Letter from Susan Mary to Joe Alsop, May 8, 1975, JA and SA Papers, box 224.
4. Undated letter from Susan Mary to Joe Alsop, probably May 1975, JA and SA Papers, box 224.
5. Letter from Susan Mary to Marietta Tree, June 4, 1975, Radcliffe.
6. Ibid.
7. Ibid.
8. Antonia Fraser, "So Chic, So True, So Sad," *Evening Standard*, March 16, 1976.
9. Letter from Susan Mary to Marietta Tree, November 19, 1975, Radcliffe.
10. Ibid.
11. Ibid.
12. Cited in a letter from Susan Mary to Marinette Berry, September 24, 1976, Sulzberger Archives.

13. Ibid.

14. Letter from Susan Mary to Marinette Berry, November 5, 1976, Sulzberger Archives.

15. Ibid.

16. Walter Isaacson, *Kissinger: A Biography* (New York: Simon & Schuster, 1992), 722.

17. Letter from Susan Mary to Marinette Berry, November 12, 1977, Sulzberger Archives.

18. Letter from Susan Mary to Marinette Berry, December 19, 1976, Sulzberger Archives.

19. Letter from Susan Mary to Marinette Berry, March 14, 1977.

20. Letter from Susan Mary to Duff Cooper, April 6, 1951.

21. Letter from Joe Alsop to Susan Mary, August 23, 1976, JA and SA Papers, box 224.

22. Letter from Susan Mary to Joe Alsop, January 10, 1978, JA and SA Papers, box 224.

23. Charlotte Hays, "Lunch with Nancy," *Washingtonian,* November 1981.

24. Letter from Susan Mary to Marietta Tree, April 9, 1982.

25. Letter from Susan Mary to Joe Alsop, June 18, 1986, JA and SA Papers, box 224.

26. Ibid.

27. Susan Mary Alsop, *Yankees at the Court: The First Americans in Paris* (New York: Doubleday, 1982), 65.

28. Letter from Susan Mary to Joe Alsop, September 19, 1980, JA and SA Papers, box 224.

29. Susan Watters, "Alsop's Fables," *Women's Wear Daily,* November 4, 1983.

30. Letter from Selwa Roosevelt to Susan Mary, September 23, 1988, JA and SA Papers, box 224.

31. Susan Mary Alsop, introduction to Edith Wharton, *Madame de Treymes and Three Novellas* (New York: Macmillan, 1987).

32. This drypoint print was commissioned from the painter Vidal-Quadras by Pierre Bordeaux-Groult.

33. Letter from Susan Mary to Joe Alsop, June 27, 1980, JA and SA Papers, box 224.

34. Postcard from Susan Mary to Sybil Patten, September 18, 1988.

X. AND NIGHT CAME

1. Joseph Alsop and Adam Platt, *"I've Seen the Best of It": Memoirs* (New York: Norton, 1992), 469.

2. Letter from Susan Mary to her son, May 11, 1990.

3. Letter from Susan Mary to Anne de Rougemont, December 9, 1989, Rougemont Archives.

4. Letter from Susan Mary to Cy Sulzberger, January 2, 1991, Sulzberger Archives.

5. Letter from Susan Mary to Marietta Tree, April 9, 1982.

6. Maureen Dowd, "On Washington; The WASP Descendancy," *New York Times,* October 31, 1993.

7. Ibid. This omission would be made up for a few years later. After Hillary Clinton left the White House, she invited Susan Mary and Paige Rense to lunch, along with the decorators Rodd Brown and Todd Davis. Former President Clinton came to see Susan Mary when lunch was over, but Susan Mary was in a bad mood because her companions had kept her from smoking at the table.

8. Letter from Susan Mary to Duff Cooper, October 1, 1951.

9. Sidney Blumenthal, "The Ruins of Georgetown," *New Yorker,* October 21–28, 1996.

Sources and Bibliography

The main sources for this book have been the letters, photographs, albums, and articles generously made available to me by William S. Patten, Susan Mary Alsop's son. To these must be added the five hundred love letters written by Susan Mary to Duff Cooper between 1947 and 1953 and rediscovered by Duff and Diana Cooper's granddaughter, Artemis Cooper. John Julius Norwich, their son, allowed me to use this remarkable unpublished correspondence. Lord Norwich also allowed me to read the unpublished parts of his father's diary.

Sylvia Blake, Anne de Rougemont, and David Sulzberger also lent me unpublished letters from Susan Mary Alsop.

I also consulted documents in the following archives:

The Central Intelligence Agency Online for Joseph Alsop's file, declassified under the Freedom of Information Act

The John Fitzgerald Kennedy Library Online (The Oral History Project's recorded interviews with Hervé Alphand, Joseph W. Alsop, and Sir Isaiah Berlin, and the White House Diary)

The Joseph Alsop and Stewart Alsop Papers in the Library of Congress

The Marietta Tree Papers in the Arthur and Elizabeth Schlesinger Library on the History of Women in America at Harvard University's Radcliffe Institute for Advanced Study

BOOKS BY SUSAN MARY ALSOP

Alsop, Susan Mary. *The Congress Dances*. New York: Harper & Row, 1984.
———. *Lady Sackville: A Biography*. New York: Doubleday, 1978.
———. *To Marietta from Paris, 1945–1960*. New York: Doubleday, 1975.
———. *Yankees at the Court: The First Americans in Paris*. New York: Doubleday, 1982.

HISTORICAL STUDIES

Abdy, Jane, and Charlotte Gere. *The Souls*. London: Sidgwick and Jackson, 1984.
Aldrich, Nelson W. *Old Money: The Mythology of America's Upper Class*. New York: Knopf, 1988.
Almquist, Leann Grabavoy. *Joseph Alsop and American Foreign Policy: The Journalist as Advocate*. Lanham, Md.: University Press of America, 1993.
Aron, Raymond. *République impériale: Les États-Unis dans le monde, 1945–1972*. Paris: Calman-Lévy, 1973.
Azema, Jean-Pierre. *De Munich à la Libération, 1938–1944*. Paris: Seuil, 1979.
Beevor, Antony, and Artemis Cooper. *Paris after the Liberation*. New York: Doubleday, 1994.
Behrman, Greg. *The Most Noble Adventure: The Marshall Plan and the Time When America Helped Save Europe*. New York: Simon & Schuster, 2007.
Burt, Nathaniel. *First Families—The Making of an American Aristocracy*. Boston: Little, Brown & Co., 1970.
Charmley, John. *Churchill's Grand Alliance: The Anglo-American Special Relationship, 1940–1957*. London: Hodder & Stoughton, 1995.
Cooper, Artemis. *Cairo in the War, 1939–1945*. London: Hamish Hamilton, 1989.
Girault, René, Robert Frank, and Jacques Thobie. *La lois des géants, 1941–1964*. Paris: Masson, 1993.
Glass, Charles. *Americans in Paris: Life and Death Under Nazi Occupation*. London: HarperPress, 2009.
Hennessy, Peter. *Having It So Good: Britain in the Fifties*. London: Penguin, 2007.
Hennessy, Peter. *Never Again: Britain, 1945–1951*. London: Penguin, 2006.
Hitchcock, William. *The Struggle for Europe*. New York: Anchor Books, 2004.
Kennedy, Roger G. *Orders from France: The Americans and the French in a Revolutionary World, 1780–1820*. New York: Knopf, 1989.
Kersaudy, François. *De Gaulle et Churchill*. Paris: Perrin, 2003.

Krout, John A., and Arnold S. Rice. *United States History from 1865.* New York: HarperCollins, 1991.

Lacorne, Denis, Jacques Rupnik, and Marie-France Toinet. *L'Amérique dans les têtes: Un siècle de fascination et d'aversion.* Paris: Hachette, 1986.

Lacorne, Denis, and Justin Vaïsse. *La Présidence impériale: De Franklin D. Roosevelt à George Bush.* Paris: Odile Jacob, 2007.

Lacour-Gayet, Robert. *Histoire des États-Unis.* Paris: Fayard, 1976.

Masters, Brian. *The Dukes: The Origins, Ennoblement and History of 26 Families.* London: Blond and Briggs, 1980.

Matthiex, Jean, and René Vincent. *"Aujourd'hui", 1945–1990.* Paris: Masson, 1994.

Mee, Charles L., Jr. *The Marshall Plan: The Launching of the Pax Americana.* New York: Simon & Schuster, 1984.

Olson, Lynne. *Troublesome Young Men: The Churchill Conspiracy of 1940.* London: Bloomsbury, 2008.

Paxton, Robert O. *La France de Vichy, 1940–1944.* Paris: Seuil, 1973.

Perkins, James Breck. *France in the American Revolution.* New York: Houghton Mifflin, 1911.

Pugh, Martin. *"We Danced All Night": A Social History of Britain between the Wars.* London: Bodley Head, 2008.

Reich, Charles A. *The Greening of America: How the Youth Revolution Is Trying to Make America Livable.* New York: Random House, 1970.

Rioux, Jean-Pierre. *La France de la Quatrième République. Vol. 1, L'ardeur et la nécessité (1944–1952).* Paris: Seuil, 1980.

———. *La France de la Quatrième République. Vol. 2, L'expansion et l'impuissance (1952–1958).* Paris: Seuil, 1983.

Roncayolo, Marcel. *Histoire du monde contemporain. Vol. 3, Depuis 1939.* Paris: Bordas, 1973.

Rorabaugh, W. J. *Kennedy and the Promise of the Sixties.* Cambridge: Cambridge University Press, 2002.

Safire, William. *Before the Fall: An Inside View of the Pre-Watergate White House.* New York: Doubleday, 1975.

Salk, Susanna. *Celebrating Wasp Style: A Privileged Life.* New York: Assouline, 2007.

Sirinelli, Jean-François. *La France de 1914 à nos jours.* Paris: PUF, 1993.

Trotignon, Yves. *La France au XXe siècle.* Paris: Bordas, 1968.

MEMOIRS, LETTERS, AND BIOGRAPHIES

Acheson, Dean. *Present at the Creation: My Years in the State Department.* New York: Norton, 1969.

Alsop, Joseph W. *FDR: A Centenary Remembrance*. New York: Viking, 1982.

———, and Stewart Alsop. *The Reporter's Trade*. New York: Reynal, 1958.

———, and Adam Platt. *"I've Seen the Best of It": Memoirs*. New York: Norton, 1992.

Alsop, Stewart. *The Center: Power and People in Political Washington*. New York: Harper & Row, 1968.

———. *Stay of Execution: A Sort of Memoir*. Philadelphia: Lippincott, 1973.

Anthony, Carl Sferrazza. *The Kennedy White House: Family Life and Pictures, 1961–1963*. New York: Simon & Schuster, 2001.

Beadle, Betty. *Power at Play: A Memoir of Parties, Politicians, and the Presidents in my Bedroom*. Washington, D.C.: Regnery Gateway, 1993.

Beaton, Cecil. *The Unexpurgated Beaton: The Cecil Beaton Diaries as He Wrote Them*. London: Weidenfelt and Nicolson, 2002.

Bemelmans, Ludwig. *Holiday in France*. London: Andre Deutsch, 1958.

Benaïm, Laurence. *Marie-Laure de Noailles: la vicomtesse du bizarre*. Paris: Grasset, 2001.

Berlin, Isaiah. *Enlightening: Letters, 1946–1951*. Edited by Henry Hardy and Jennifer Holmes. London: Chatto and Windus, 2009.

———. *Personal Impressions*. London: Hogarth, 1981.

Birmingham, Stephen. *Jacqueline Bouvier Kennedy Onassis*. New York: Grosset and Dunlop, 1978.

Bohlen, Charles E. *Witness to History, 1929–1969*. New York: Norton, 1973.

Botsford, Gardner. *A Life of Privilege, Mostly*. London: Granta, 2007.

Bradford, Sarah. *America's Queen: The Life of Jacqueline Kennedy Onassis*. New York: Penguin, 2001.

Bradlee, Benjamin C. *Conversations with Kennedy*. New York: Norton, 1975.

———. *A Good Life: Newspapering and Other Adventures*. New York: Simon & Schuster, 1995.

Brenner, Marie. *Great Dames: What I Learned from Older Women*. New York: Crown, 2000.

Brokaw, Tom. *Boom! Voices of the Sixties: Personal Reflections on the '60s and Today*. New York: Random House, 2007.

Bundy, McGeorge. *Danger and Survival: Choices About the Bomb in the First Fifty Years*. New York: Random House, 1988.

Burleigh, Nina. *A Very Private Woman: The Life and Unsolved Murder of Presidential Mistress Mary Meyer*. New York: Bantam, 1998.

Caro, Robert A. *The Years of Lyndon Johnson: Master of the Senate*. New York: Knopf, 2002.

Charmley, John. *Churchill, the End of Glory: A Political Biography*. London: Hodder & Stoughton, 1993.

———. *Duff Cooper: The Authorized Biography.* London: Weidenfeld and Nicolson, 1986.

Child, Julia, and Alex Prud'homme. *My Life in France.* New York: Knopf, 2006.

Cocteau, Jean. *Journal, 1942–1945.* Edited by Jean Touzot. Paris: Gallimard, 1989.

———. *Lettre aux Américains.* Paris: Grasset, 1949.

———. *Le Passé défini.* Vol. 1, *1951–1952.* Paris: Gallimard, 1983.

Cooke, Alistair. *Reporting America: The Life of the Nation, 1946–2004.* London: Penguin, 2008.

Cooper, Artemis. *The Diana Cooper Scrapbook.* London: Hamish Hamilton, 1987.

———. *Writing at the Kitchen Table: The Authorized Biography of Elizabeth David.* London: Michael Joseph, 1999.

Cooper, Diana. *Autobiography.* Salisbury: Michael Russell, 1979.

———, and Duff Cooper. *A Durable Fire: The Letters of Duff and Diana Cooper, 1913–1950.* Edited by Artemis Cooper. London: Hamish Hamilton, 1983.

Cooper, Duff. *The Duff Cooper Diaries.* Edited by John Julius Norwich. London: Phoenix, 2006.

———. *Old Men Forget: The Biography of Duff Cooper.* London: Rupert Hart-Davis, 1953.

———. *Operation Heartbreak.* London: Rupert Hart-Davis, 1950.

———. *Talleyrand.* London: Phoenix, 1997.

Cordery, Stacy A. *Alice: Alice Roosevelt Longworth from White House Princess to Washington Power Broker.* New York: Viking, 2007.

Dallek, Robert. *An Unfinished Life: John F. Kennedy, 1917–1963.* Boston: Little, Brown & Co., 2003.

Deharme, Lise. *Les années perdues.* Paris: Plon, 1961.

Devonshire, Deborah. *Home to Roost and Other Peckings.* Edited by Charlotte Mosley. London: John Murray, 2009.

———. *Wait for Me! Memoirs of the Youngest Mitford Sister.* Edited by Charlotte Mosley. London: John Murray, 2010.

Dewey, Peter. *As They Were.* New York: Beechhurst Press, 1946.

Didion, Joan. *L'Amérique: Choroniques.* Paris: Grasset, 2009.

———. *We Tell Ourselves Stories in Order to Live: Collected Nonfiction.* New York: Knopf, 2006.

Diesbach, Ghislain de. *La Princesse Bibesco, 1886–1973.* Paris: Perrin, 1986.

Dowd, Maureen. *Are Men Necessary? When Sexes Collide.* New York: G. P. Putnam's Sons, 2005.

Duteurtre, Benoît. *Ballets roses.* Paris: Grasset, 2009.

Enthoven, Jean-Paul. *La Dernière Femme*. Paris: Grasset et Fasquelle, 2006.

Ernaux, Annie. *Les Années*. Paris: Gallimard, 2008.

Faucigny-Lucinge, Jean-Louis. *Un gentilhomme cosmopolite*. Paris: Perrin, 1990.

Fitch, Noel Riley. *Sylvia Beach and the Lost Generation: A History of Literary Paris in the Twenties and Thirties*. London: Souvenir Press, 1984.

Flanner, Janet. *Paris Journal, 1944–1955*. New York: Harcourt, 1988.

———. *Paris Journal, 1956–1965*. New York: Harcourt, 1988.

———. *Paris Was Yesterday, 1925–1939*. Edited by Irving Drutman. London: Virago, 2003.

Fleming, Ann. *The Letters of Ann Fleming*. Edited by Mark Amory. London: Collins, 1985.

Forestier, François. *Marilyn et JFK*. Paris: Albin Michel, 2008.

Galey, Matthieu. *Journal I, 1953–1973*. Paris: Grasset, 1987.

Gladwyn, Cynthia. *The Diaries of Cynthia Gladwyn*. Edited by Miles Jebb. London: Constable, 1995.

———. *The Paris Embassy*. London: Collins, 1976.

Gladwyn, Hubert Miles. *The Memoirs of Lord Gladwyn*. London: Weidenfelt and Nicolson, 1972.

Gopnik, Adam, ed. *Americans in Paris: A Literary Anthology*. New York: Library of America, 2004.

Goulaine, Robert de. *Paris 60*. Monaco: Motifs, 2006.

Graham, Katharine. *Katharine Graham's Washington*. New York: Vintage, 2003.

———. *Personal History*. New York: Vintage, 1998.

Green, Julien. *Paris*. Paris: Fayard, 1995.

Halberstam, David. *The Best and the Brightest*. New York: Ballantine, 1993.

———. *The Fifties*. New York: Villard, 1993.

Haslam, Nicholas. *Redeeming Features: A Memoir*. New York: Knopf, 2009.

Hastings, Selina. *Nancy Mitford*. London: Papermac, 1986.

Henderson, Nicholas. *The Private Office*. London: Weidenfeld and Nicolson, 1984.

Hersch, Seymour M. *The Dark Side of Camelot*. Boston: Little, Brown & Company, 1997.

Heyman, C. David. *Bobby and Jackie*. New York: Atria, 2009.

———. *The Georgetown Ladies' Social Club: Power, Passion, and Politics in the Nation's Capital*. New York: Atria, 2003.

———. *A Woman Named Jackie* (TV miniseries). Carol Communications, 1989.

Hughes, Philippe d'. *Chronique buissonière des années cinquante*. Paris: de Fallois, 2008.

Isaacson, Walter. *Kissinger: A Biography*. New York: Simon & Schuster, 1992.

———, and Edward Thomas. *The Wise Men: Six Friends and the World They Made*. New York: Simon & Schuster, 1986.

Jardin, Pascal. *La guerre à neuf ans*. Paris: Grasset et Fasquelle, 2005.

Joder, Edwin M., Jr. *Joe Alsop's War: A Study of Journalistic Influence and Intrigue*. Chapel Hill: University of North Carolina Press, 1995.

Kaplan, Justin. *When the Astors Owned New York: Blue Bloods and Grand Hotels in a Gilded Age*. New York: Viking, 2006.

Kaplan, Leslie. *Mon Amérique commence en Pologne*. Paris: P.O.L., 2009.

Karnow, Stanley. *Paris in the Fifties*. New York: Random House, 1997.

———. *Vietnam in History*. New York: Viking, 1983.

Kennan, George F. *Sketches from a Life*. New York: Pantheon, 1989.

Kennedy, John F. *"Let the Word Go Forth": The Speeches, Statements, and Writings of John F. Kennedy, 1947–1963*. Edited by Theodore S. Sorensen. New York: Delacorte, 1988.

Kennedy, Robert. *Thirteen Days: A Memoir of the Cuban Missile Crisis*. New York: New American Library, 1969.

Kiplinger, Austin H., and Knight A. Kiplinger. *Washington Now*. New York: Harper & Row, 1975.

Kissinger, Henry. *The White House Years*. Boston: Little, Brown & Co., 1979.

Lasky, Victor. *JFK: The Man and the Myth*. New York: Macmillan, 1969.

Lees-Milne, James. *Harold Nicolson: A Biography, 1930–1968*. London: Chatto and Windus, 1981.

Leslie, Anita. *Edwardians in Love*. London: Hutchison, 1973.

Lewis, R. W. B. *Edith Wharton: A Biography*. New York: Fromm, 1985.

Mahoney, Richard D. *Sons and Brothers: The Days of Jack and Bobby Kennedy*. New York: Arcade, 1999.

Mahoney, Rosemary. *A Likely Story: One Summer with Lillian Hellman*. New York: Doubleday, 1998.

Mailer, Norman. *The Time of Our Time*. New York: Abacus, 1999.

Manchester, William. *The Death of a President: November 1963*. New York: Harper & Row, 1967.

———. *The Last Lion: Winston Spencer Churchill Alone, 1932–1934*. Boston: Little, Brown & Co., 1988.

Merry, Robert W. *Taking on the World: Joseph and Stewart Alsop, Guardians of the American Century*. New York: Viking, 1996.

Millau, Christian. *Paris m'a dit: années 50, fin d'une époque*. Paris: de Fallois, 2000.

Mitford, Nancy. *Une Anglaise à Paris: Chroniques*. Paris: Payot et Rivages, 2008.

———. *The Letters of Nancy Mitford and Evelyn Waugh*. Edited by Charlotte Mosley. London: Hodder & Stoughton, 1996.

———. *Love from Nancy: The Letters of Nancy Mitford*. Edited by Charlotte Mosely. London: Hodder & Stoughton, 1993.

Moorhead, Lucy. *Entertaining in Washington*. New York: G. P. Putnam's Sons, 1978.

Mosley, Charlotte, ed., *The Mitfords: Letters Between Six Sisters*. New York: HarperCollins, 2007.

Mosley, Diana. *The Pursuit of Laughter*. London: Gibson Square, 2009.

Nicolson, Harold. *Diaries and Letters, 1945–1962*. Edited by Nigel Nicolson. London: Collins, 1968.

Nicolson, Nigel. *Long Life*. New York: G. P. Putnam's Sons, 1998.

———. *Portrait of a Marriage*. London: Weidenfeld and Nicolson, 1973.

Norwich, John Julius. *Trying to Please*. Dorset, United Kingdom: Dovecote Press, 2008.

O'Brien, Michael. *John F. Kennedy: A Biography*. New York: Thomas Dunne, 2005.

Ogden, Christopher. *The Life of the Party: The Biography of Pamela Churchill Hayward Harriman*. London: Warner, 1995.

Patten, William S. *My Three Fathers and the Elegant Deceptions of My Mother, Susan Mary Alsop*. New York: PublicAffairs, 2008.

Reeves, Richard. *President Kennedy: Profile of Power*. New York: Simon & Schuster, 1993.

Sackville-West, Vita. *Pepita*. London: Hogarth Press, 1937.

Sagan, Françoise. *Bonjour New York*. Paris: L'Herne, 2007.

Schlesinger, Arthur M., Jr. *Journals, 1955–2000*. New York: Penguin Press, 2007.

———. *A Life in the Twentieth Century: Innocent Beginnings, 1917–1950*. New York: Houghton Mifflin, 2002.

———. *A Thousand Days: John F. Kennedy in the White House*. Boston: Houghton Mifflin, 1965.

Seebohm, Caroline. *No Regrets: The Life of Marietta Tree*. New York: Simon & Schuster, 1997.

Smith, Sally Bedell. *Grace and Power: The Private World of the Kennedy White House*. New York: Random House, 2004.

———. *In All His Glory: The Life of W. S. Paley*. New York: Simon & Schuster, 1990.

———. *Reflected Glory: The Life of Pamela Churchill Harriman*. New York: Simon & Schuster, 1996.

Soames, Mary. *Clementine Churchill*. London: Cassel, 1979.

Sorensen, Theodore C. *Kennedy*. New York: Harper & Row, 1965.

Spade and Archer. *Spade and Archer's 50 Maps of Washington D.C.* New York: Spade and Archer, 1965.

Steel, Ronald. *Walter Lippman and the American Century.* Boston: Little, Brown & Co., 1980.

Sterba, Jim. *Frankie's Place: A Love Story.* New York: Grove Press, 2003.

Styron, William. *Havanas in Camelot.* New York: Random House, 2008.

Sulzberger, C. L. *The Last of the Giants.* New York: Macmillan, 1970.

———. *Seven Continents and Forty Years: A Concentration of Memoirs.* New York: Quadrangle, 1977.

Sulzberger, Marina. *Letters and Diaries of Marina Sulzberger.* Edited by C. L. Sulzberger. New York: Crown, 1978.

Talbott, Strobe. *The Master of the Game: Paul Nitze and the Nuclear Peace.* New York: Knopf, 1988.

Thomas, Evan. *Very Best Men: Four Who Dared, The Early Years of the CIA.* New York: Simon & Schuster, 1995.

Thompson, Laura. *Life in a Cold Climate: Nancy Mitford, A Portrait of a Contradictory Woman.* London: Review, 2003.

Vickers, Hugo. *Cecil Beaton: The Authorized Biography.* London: Weidenfeld and Nicolson, 1985.

Vidal, Gore. *Palimpsest.* London: Abacus, 2006.

———. *Point to Point Navigation: A Memoir, 1964 to 2006.* London, Abacus, 2007.

Vilmorin, Louise de. *Correspondance avec ses amis.* Edited by Olivier Muth. Paris: Gallimard, 2008.

———. *Intimités.* Edited by Patrick Mauriès. Paris: Gallimard, 2001.

———, Duff Cooper, and Diana Cooper. *Correspondance à trois, 1944–1953.* Edited by Olivier Muth. Paris: Gallimard, 2008.

Wagener, Françoise. *Je suis née inconsolable: Louise de Vilmorin (1902–1969).* Paris: Albin Michel, 2008.

Waugh, Evelyn, and Diana Cooper. *Mr. Wu and Mrs. Stitch: The Letters of Evelyn Waugh and Diana Cooper.* Edited by Artemis Cooper. London: Sceptre, 1992.

Weber, Ronald. *News of Paris: American Journalists in the City of Light Between the Wars.* Chicago: Ivan R. Dee, 2006.

White, Edmund. *Our Paris: Sketches from Memory.* New York: Knopf, 1995.

Whitehouse, C. S. *Then and Now: Memoirs of C. S. Whitehouse.* Marshall, Va.: s.n., 2001.

Wofford, Harris. *Of Kennedys and Kings: Making Sense of the Sixties.* New York: Farrar, Straus and Giroux, 1980.

Zamoyski, Adam. *Rites of Peace: The Fall of Napoleon and the Congress of Vienna.* London: HarperPress, 2007.

Ziegler, Philip. *Diana Cooper.* London: Hamish Hamilton, 1981.

NOVELS, PLAYS, AND SHORT STORIES

Auchincloss, Louis. *Her Infinite Variety.* Boston: Houghton Mifflin, 2000.
———. *Honorable Men.* Boston: Houghton Mifflin, 1985.
———. *Manhattan Monologues.* Boston: Houghton Mifflin, 2002.
———. *The Rector of Justin.* Boston: Houghton Mifflin, 2002.
Buchwald, Art. *Counting Sheep.* New York: G. P. Putnam's Sons, 1969.
Capote, Truman. *Music for Chameleons.* New York: Signet, 1981.
Cheever, John. *The Stories of John Cheever.* New York: Vintage International, 2000.
Cortanze, Gérard de. *De Gaulle en maillot de bain.* Paris: Plon, 2007.
Ellroy, James. *American Tabloid.* New York: Knopf, 1995.
Enard, Jean-Pierre. *La Reine du Technicolor.* Bordeaux: Finitude, 2008.
Faulks, Sebastien. *On Green Dolphin Street.* New York: Vintage International, 2001.
Fitzgerald, F. Scott. *Tender Is the Night.* London: Penguin, 1998.
———. *This Side of Paradise.* New York: Scribner's, 1921.
Hemingway, Ernest. *The Sun Also Rises.* New York: Scribner Classics, 1996.
Hitchcock, Jane Stanton. *Social Crimes.* New York: Miramax, 2003.
James, Henry. *The Ambassadors.* London: Penguin Books, 1996.
Mallon, Thomas. *Fellow Travelers.* New York: Vintage Books, 2008.
Maxwell, William. *The Château.* London: Harvill Press, 2001.
Mitford, Nancy. *The Nancy Mitford Omnibus.* London: Penguin Books, 2001.
Morand, Paul. *Fin de siècle.* Paris: Gallimard, 2008.
Morand, Paul. *Venises.* Paris: Gallimard, 1971.
Powell, Dawn. *Une époque exquise.* Paris: Quai Voltaire, 2009.
Vidal, Gore. *Empire.* London: Abacus, 2003.
———. *The Golden Age.* London: Abacus, 2001.
———. *Washington, D.C.* London: Abacus, 2004.
Wharton, Edith. *The Age of Innocence.* New York: Barnes & Noble, 1996.
———. *Madame de Treymes and Three Novellas* (introduction by Susan Mary Alsop). New York: Collier, 1987.
———. *The New York Stories of Edith Wharton.* New York: New York Review Books, 2007.

The magazine and newspaper articles consulted during the research for this book are not listed, but I would like to mention Susan Braudy's article on Susan Mary Alsop, "Camelot's Second Lady," in the February 2006 issue of *Vanity Fair.*

Index